PALIMPSEST

PALIMPSEST
DOCUMENTS FROM A KOREAN ADOPTION
Lisa Wool-Rim Sjöblom 정 물 림

TRANSLATED BY
Hanna Strömberg,
Lisa Wool-Rim Sjöblom,
and Richey Wyver

Drawn & Quarterly

Many of the names in this album have been changed, and certain people are not named, in order to protect identities. For the same reason, some personal details have been altered. The people who appear with their real names have given their consent.

The album contains footnotes, marked by asterisks.
The footnotes are collected at the end of the book.

The cost of this translation was defrayed by a subsidy from the Swedish Arts Council, gratefully acknowledged.

drawnandquarterly.com

978-1-77046-330-1
First edition: October 2019
Printed in China
10 9 8 7 6 5 4 3 2 1

Cataloguing data available from Library and Archives Canada

Published in the USA by Drawn & Quarterly,
a client publisher of Farrar, Straus and Giroux

Published in Canada by Drawn & Quarterly,
a client publisher of Raincoast Books

Published in the United Kingdom by Drawn & Quarterly,
a client publisher of Publishers Group UK

This album is dedicated to all adoptees
—living and dead—
whose voices have been silenced

Palimpsest:
A very old text or document in which writing has been removed and covered or replaced by new writing.

Adoption:
The act of legally taking a child to be taken care of as your own.

—Cambridge Dictionary

Stockholm
September 21st, 1994

Dear Mr. Sjöblom,

You called me just over a week ago to ask if it was possible to find out more about your daughter Lisa from Korea. I promised to speak to Ms. Kang, who was here visiting us, and I have now done so.

Ms. Kang told me that the older the adoptees are, the harder it is to find information on them. There were no computers back then and it wasn't mandatory to register the social security numbers of the birth parents, etc.

When searching for a person who has relinquished their child to an organization for international adoption, the following is done:

· A telegram is sent to the address in the adoption file.

· If it is returned to SWS, they contact the "dong office," which is an office located on every block, to ask if they have any information about where the person you're searching for has moved to.

· If the "dong office" doesn't have any information, SWS contacts the "ku office," which is an office located in every city district. They keep registers of the people living there.

· If they don't have any information either, the police will be contacted for the social security number or date of birth of the person you're looking for. Sometimes the social security number and date of birth turn out to be false. The address might also be false, perhaps it is just the name of a mountain with a number added.

Naturally, if a woman has to relinquish her child, she wouldn't want anyone to know that she had even been pregnant. Even nowadays, it's very hard for single mothers to get by, and it was even worse some time ago. A single mother would have had little chance to stay with her family, and the possibility of getting married would have been non-existent.

Korea is a tough society. Economically, the country recovered rapidly after the war, but many people had to pay a high price for this. The social rules are very strict and those who don't fit in become outcasts.

I understand that this is a difficult answer for Lisa, but I'm afraid it's the only one I can give her. I've worked with SWS for fifteen years, and I visited Korea for the first time in 1971. I can guarantee that they've done everything in their power to help Lisa.

However, they still have Lisa's file, and if anyone comes to search for her, we will be notified, and they also will be told about Lisa's own inquiries. But chances are that Lisa's mother hadn't told anyone about Lisa's birth or adoption, and we can only hope that Lisa's mother today has a family, a husband, and children. A revelation of Lisa's existence would most likely break up that family and cause even more people pain.

I am convinced that Lisa's mother didn't have any other choice, either for herself or for Lisa, when she decided upon adoption. I'm also convinced that Lisa's mother has not forgotten her; it's just that we don't know where her mother is with her thoughts.

I hope Lisa can accept these facts and still embrace Korea as her first country, a wonderful, beautiful country that I hope you and she will some day be able to visit.

Kind Regards,
Margareta Blomkvist,
*Adoptionscentrum**

PART 1 Scriptio Superior

I'm better prepared this time.

So, when did you have your last period?

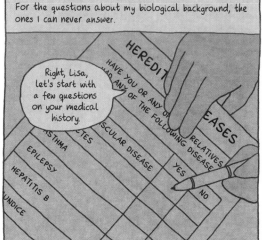

For the questions about my biological background, the ones I can never answer.

Right, Lisa, let's start with a few questions on your medical history.

HEREDIT...
HAVE YOU OR ANY O...
HAD ANY OF THE FOLLOWING DISEASE...
RELATIVES
...EASES
...TES
...SCULAR DISEASE
ASTHMA
EPILEPSY
HEPATITIS B
...UNDICE
YES
NO

Do you know anything about your mom's pregnancy and your own birth? If not, you might want to talk to her. It can be good preparation, because it can give you an idea of what to expect.

Last time, these questions tore open deep wounds that I thought had healed a long time ago.

During my first pregnancy, these questions reminded me that this body of mine is a mystery. An enigma.

That I'm a person who manifested out of thin air, a person without roots. Not born, but still here.

When I found out I was expecting my first child, it was as though my mythological mother entered my body and soul.

It felt as though I was carrying her, not my son.

It was then that I realized, much to my shock, that my life had started in another person's womb, another person's body.

Was my mother as shocked as I was?

When she understood the condition she was in?

Was she scared? Was she lonely?

It's no wonder we adoptees forget that we were ever born. We're taught that our existence began the day we met our new families.

Where do babies come from?

Arlanda airport!

The word that describes how we become a part of our families hides the fact that we ever belonged to another one.

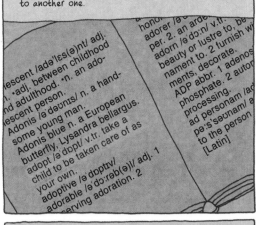

This is the origin story I grew up with. It was put up on my parents' fridge as a poem.*

Not flesh of my flesh
Nor bone of my bone,
But still miraculously
my own.
Never forget for a
single minute,
You didn't grow under
my heart
But in it.

Don't forget

Yogurt
Milk
Cheese
Eggs

Many of us actually believe that our lives started with a flight.

It was as if you'd been away on a trip and then came back— to us.

Our first families are eventually reduced to the margins

A mother is not the woman who just gave birth to you, but the one who raised and took care of you!

to be completely erased in the end.

The important thing is that you're here now!

Many adoptees feel an inexplicable grief on their birthdays. They somehow remind us of a loss that no one will talk about.

We mourn in silence. We don't want to risk upsetting or hurting our adoptive parents, so when our losses are talked about as a positive, we keep quiet.

I'm sure your mom loved you, but she gave you away to give you a better life.

We become an empty vessel for other people to fill with their own story.

It's much better that they can come here, instead of growing up in those horrible orphanages!

Eventually, we start retelling those myths we've been fed ourselves.

Since my parents couldn't have children of their own, they turned to adoption.

And after a while, our first families disappear completely from our own stories. And so do we.

The nice thing about being adopted is that you know you're wanted, maybe even more than other kids are. I mean, it's not like we came here by mistake, our parents had to really fight to get us here.

Over the years, the story has worn a hole in my soul.

During the pushing stage at the birth of my first child, it seemed that my body was possessed by my mother. She was me, and I was the child on my way out into the world. It is recommended that you use visualization techniques to help you through the demanding labor. Each contraction, however painful, brings you closer to your baby.

But what do you do when the contractions are pulling you away from it?

They're going to take my baby! They're going to take my baby!

You're doing fine, Lisa! Just don't forget to breathe! It'll soon be time to push... You're doing great!

And the baby inside is going to be given to someone else?

I was taken from my mother as a newborn. Was she even allowed to hold me?

울랄람!

An image of that separation has been stored in my body for all those years, and now it throws me into total darkness.

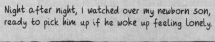

Night after night, I watched over my newborn son, ready to pick him up if he woke up feeling lonely.

Each cry tore me apart. I thought he sounded like an abandoned child.

Sssh, sssh, honey, Mommy's here! Mommy's here! I'm here!

I was tormented by nightmare visions, in which I die and Teddy is taken away to an orphanage...

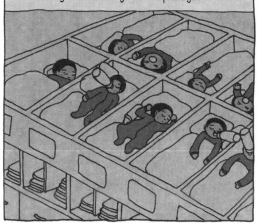

to later be adopted and taught to forget that I'd ever been his mother.

Sven, your mom couldn't take care of you, so she gave you away so that you could have a better life.

I thought about the little child I once was. Who lived in Korea, who was Wool Rim.* Who was Korean, who spoke Korean. Who may have been abandoned, but was still part of something bigger...

who was put on a plane with a one-way ticket to Sweden, accompanied by an escort who didn't look like anyone she'd ever seen before...

who landed in a foreign land, where she was handed over to complete strangers...

where there were no familiar tastes or smells...

where she couldn't comprehend a word anybody said. Where nobody understood her...

제 말 좀 들어보세요!

제 말 좀 들어보세요! 아무도 내 말 이해 못해?!

where Chung Wool Rim ended and someone called Lisa began.

When Teddy refused to breastfeed, I was devastated. Once again, I felt rejected by my own flesh and blood.

Come on! Just try a little bit more! Just a bit more!

It was hard for us to form a bond, and Teddy only wanted his dad.

WAAAAH

I'd read about the benefits of breastfeeding. How irreplaceable the milk is, how the close contact builds healthy, secure children.

I wasn't breastfed but I'm still alive…

I refused to give up.

Oh! Don't let go now. Eat some more!

Come on, sweetie!

I went to a breastfeeding clinic, but they only made me feel worse.

Can't we bottle-feed him? He doesn't want to do this, he just refuses every time.

Well, um, we usually don't recommend that. The very best thing for your baby is to keep trying to breastfeed him. You just have to give it some time.

After three months of a painful and futile struggle, I reluctantly gave up and started bottle-feeding. Teddy drank happily, but I felt like a failure.

We talked about the bonding problems with nurses and a psychologist, but they just told us how nice it was that Teddy had such a close relationship with his father.

What I didn't understand at the time was that was my anxiety came from my own separation trauma.

Usually babies only want their mother. Enjoy it and get some sleep while it lasts!

It felt like yet another broken bond.

I remembered drawing family trees in school, and feeling empty inside.

Who do you come from?

For my classmates, this was a straightforward assignment. For me, though, it was like staring into a gaping abyss deep inside my body.

What are your grandparents' names?

Gunvor and Sture.

I wish I knew.

I remembered how I slowly began to understand that belonging isn't something you start feeling just because other people want you to.

While people close to me tried to make me feel that my adoption was something simple and natural, strangers did their best to complicate it.

Hi! I'm sorry, I just have to ask—where are you from?

I learned what it meant to have an appearance that does not match your name or your environment.

Come on, is it China? Or Japan?

Seriously, where are you really from? Do you understand Swedish?

There'd be a constant knot in my stomach before meeting new people, having to explain this gap between my Swedish name and my non-Swedish face.

Oh, you're Lisa? When we spoke on the phone, I didn't realize that you were

That you're you know

The knot that knows that by saying "adopted" as an explanation only leads to a barrage of intimate questions.

Were you in an orphanage? For how long?

How come your Korean parents couldn't take care of you?

How old were you when you came here?

Have you ever gone back?

Do you remember anything at all?

Do you think you have any brothers or sisters?

Do you speak Korean? Would you like to learn Korean? What was your Korean name? Do you still have that name?

Have you searched for your real family? Have you seen Spårlöst*? It's sooo good!

*"Without a Trace" is a popular Swedish TV show which follows people searching for parents or other lost relatives.

It doesn't matter what the adoptee thinks, feels, or has just said. These self-proclaimed "adoption experts" are strangers who feel entitled to ask endlessly intrusive questions before going on to share their own opinions on adoption, oblivious to their own thoughtlessness.

When I was younger, I thought it was all quite exciting, but today I feel very differently. Now, I detect another story behind this behavior. The narrative of the good country of Sweden, with its noble people, who through adoption, are saving vulnerable children of the world. Regardless of what I have to say about my own experience of being adopted, I am repeatedly told—I was lucky. I was *saved* through adoption.

21

As a kid, I fully identified as Korean, and every question about Korea just made me feel special. I compensated by being as Korean as I could.

Can I play with the hanbok again?

My best friend Jin was also adopted from Korea. We were pretty different, but it was comforting to have someone who shared a similar background, and whose reflection mirrored mine.

I wish I had double eyelids!

Oh, me too!

We secretly created biological ties to each other.

Sign here. Then we'll be real sisters!

Forever and ever!

We were proud to be us.

In my little world, I latched on to even the smallest thing that had anything to do with Korea.

LOOK! It was a Korean who made this shirt!

And when I finally got to try Korean food for the first time and began my lifelong romance with kimchi, I felt I had found the clearest evidence that I was a real Korean after all.

Om nom nom

One of the best days of my childhood was when a group of Korean teenagers visited my town for an international ice skating competition.

Some adoptive parents arranged a day of activities so that all the local Korean adoptees could meet them.

I practiced using chopsticks for a whole week so that I would fit in among the real Koreans at lunchtime.

Bring it on!

I sat next to a seventeen-year-old girl named Hae Suk. It was like meeting an idol. She taught me to write my name in Korean.

We became pen pals and wrote to each other for many years.

Through Hae Suk, I could regularly experience a piece of Korea.

In 1988, the Olympic Games were held in Korea, and I was proud about all the attention my first country was suddenly receiving. There was TV coverage about Korean food, culture, and nature.

I didn't know then that at this time, Korea was starting to gain its reputation as one of the world's leading exporters of children.*

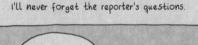

Koreana, the band who sang the official Olympic song that year, became my favorite band, largely because they were Korean, of course.

HAND IN HAND WE STAND! ♪♫

♪ ALL ACROSS ♪ THE ♫ LAND!

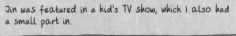

Jin was featured in a kid's TV show, which I also had a small part in.

There we are!!!

They're adopted from Korea and know Korean words and songs.

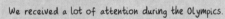

I'll never forget the reporter's questions.

What do you think about North Koreans refusing to come to the Olympics?

Jin was nine years old.

We received a lot of attention during the Olympics.

You were so good during the Olympic opening ceremony, girls! You danced so well!

Haha, he's crazy!

THANKS!!

HA HA HA

But it became more and more difficult to hold on to my Korean-ness. Over time, my pride was slowly being erased.

Ching Chong, Chinaman,
Sitting on a rail.
Along came a white man,
And chopped off
his tail!

I began believing I was ugly and that it was wrong to look like me.

Lisa, don't you understand you can't be Lucia! Your hair is black! Lucia is supposed to be blonde!

The little bubble I had been living in started to burst. The people I thought were supposed to protect me suddenly turned into the perpetrators.

NO CHINKS
ON THE BUS!!!

It was tough to keep liking my Asian face, when there weren't any role models, only caricatures.

Ching chong!

In a way it was better when there was no representation, because at least it wasn't directly offensive.

At least Ronja's got brown hair and dark eyes!

This is my Spring Scream!

In high school, what was left of my Korean pride was literally beaten out of me.

I went to school every day with my head held high. But I can't count the times...

I had to hide in the bathroom, and then run home before the end of the school day.

I had loved school more than anything. Now I was afraid to go there.

Finally, I couldn't take it anymore.

I refused to go back.

I finished high school after hours.

I moved away from home as soon as possible, and made a fresh start in a new town. In order to prevent attacks, I buried myself in books and made sure I didn't bother anyone. But this merely led to everything in me slowly but steadily being erased. Eventually, it was as if I had completely ceased to exist.

In an attempt to save myself, I asked my parents to help me find my Korean roots.

Okay then, honey. I'll contact Adoptionscentrum.

For the first time ever, I was able to read the documents that my Korean adoption agency, Social Welfare Society (SWS), had sent to my Swedish parents at the time of my adoption.

My mother was only sixteen when she had me!

Adoptionscentrum promised to contact SWS.

An answer from Korea arrived.

And it was the last I saw of myself for a long time.

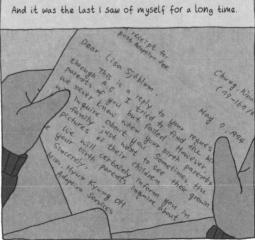

To me, being adopted didn't mean I was chosen, like others wanted me to believe. It meant I was rejected.

But you must be able to see that you were destined to be here.

I wasn't exactly planned either, but who cares?

My last dream of ever knowing my roots was crushed. It was as though they had been taken from me once more. The loss felt final.

OMMA!

I started fantasizing about death. When your life starts with adoption, there's no dust to return to. If you've never been born, you can never be fully alive.

I accepted that I was never meant to be here in this world.

Over the years, when I've tried to explain this sense of not fully existing, people have told me to stop making myself a victim

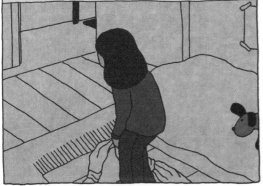

to stop blaming my adoption for everything that feels bad.

But the truth is, the story I've been telling throughout my life has been about everything but adoption.

I hadn't even considered how my adoption could mean anything

I just called to say goodbye

that it could have affected me in any way

or have grown out of a place of unimaginable pain

until the day I realized that my first biological tie was growing inside me.

Now here I am, surrounded by two little branches of the family tree that was completely bare just a few years ago.

And I promise them that I will make a new attempt to unearth the roots that the three of us grew from.

PART 2 Beneath the Surface

Twenty years have passed since the first search for my roots. This time I don't have to do it with the help of a Swedish organization. I visit the website of my Korean adoption agency, Social Welfare Services, and click on the link to their post-adoption services.

There's an online form where I can describe what I need help with. Then I sent the same inquiry via the website of Korea Adoption Services, a government institution that also does post-adoption services.

Application for Post-adoption Services

Applicant Information

Method of Application	☒ E-mail ☐ Fax ☐ Visitation ☐ Others ( )		
Name	Current Legal Name Lisa Wool-Rim Sjöblom		
	Korean (if known) CHUNG Wool Rim 정울림		
Gender	☐ Male ☒ Female	Nationality	Swedish
Birth Date		Adoption Date (Departure Date)	May 30th, 1979
Placing Agency (if known)	Social Welfare Society	Case No. (if known)	79-167/KSH
Adoptive Parents' Name			
Address	Current		
	Permanent		
Telephone No.	Home		
	C.P.		
Emergency contact			
E-mail			
Marital Status	Engaged		
Education	Higher	Occupation	Illustrator, graphic designer
Duration of stay in Korea			

Service request

I would like to get hold of all my papers regarding my adoption.
I am also searching for any of my natural family members. In my papers (see attachment) I have enclosed all the information I have been given so far.

According to my Social Study, my natural parents' names are:
Mother: Choi Sook Ja 최숙자
Father: Chung Hyo Gu 정효구

Remarks

I have attached a 12 page PDF with this e-mail. It contains my Social Study, sent to my adoptive parents, my Statement of Release for Adoption, an extract from my Korean passport and 2 photos of me, both taken at my orphanage in Korea.

Date (13/08/21):
Name: Lisa Sjöblom
Signature:

I ask my parents for the rest of my adoption papers.

Searching for a lost and hidden origin is an incredibly frustrating process. You're completely dependent upon other people's goodwill, and you're constantly trying to keep your hopes down to protect yourself from disappointment.

It's an out-of-body experience to see that the beginning of my Swedish life consists of a bunch of forms...

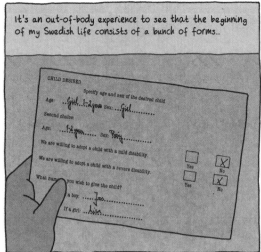

official decisions...

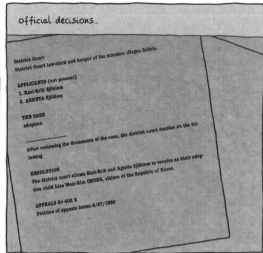

invoices, and receipts.

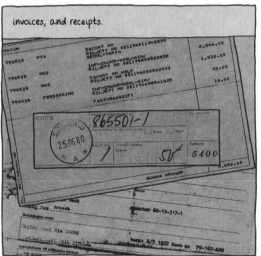

Talking about adoption as a form of child trade is completely taboo.

They say it's the adoption procedure you pay for, absolutely not the child itself.

Ha! But what's the difference?

I know! After all, the child is the whole point of the transaction.

Yeah, adoption is taking on someone else's child as your own. In the end, a bond is broken and a child is sent away, with a one-way ticket.

I find a number of letters from a Korean man, Mr. Jung, who seems to have been involved in my adoption. Dad sends me a photo of him.

He was involved in my brother's adoption as well, which was before mine. On a visit to Sweden, he met my parents and promised to find them a daughter too.

Back in Korea, he picked me, and after a few months, I was on the plane to Sweden.

So many people, authorities, and institutions were directly involved in steering my life towards Sweden. There are countless middlemen involved in an adoption.*

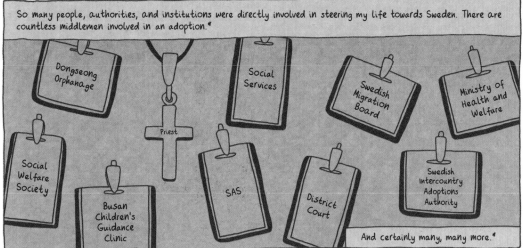

Dongseong Orphanage

Priest

Social Services

Swedish Migration Board

Ministry of Health and Welfare

Social Welfare Society

Busan Children's Guidance Clinic

SAS

District Court

Swedish Intercountry Adoptions Authority

And certainly many, many more.*

I visit the library and borrow children's books about adoptees, so that my kids can learn a little more about our background.

"And the Mom and Dad got their highest wish granted."*

Yeah, thanks to the kid losing her first parents...

I realize quickly that the books are insufferable.

Okay, we'll try this one instead!

Change again!?

Play!

The focus is always on the adoptive parents.

"In the beginning the cat was born in a land far away. He didn't have a Mom...

or Dad who could take care of him."*

What about this one?

Maybe it's because everything is written by adoptive parents.

"You thought her eyes were the kindest eyes you'd ever seen yourself reflected in... She whispered to you in a strange language that she was your mother and that she would never, ever leave you."*

No wonder it comes as such a huge shock when you start to see the cold reality of how an adoption works, as an adult.

Being chosen for adoption is actually dependent on fulfilling the right criteria. That we are cute enough, and that we have been picked out by a social worker.

And one thing no one ever mentions is how many times we were rejected, how many times we didn't meet the expectations of these potential parents.

The pile of records mainly gives me answers as to how my parents went about the adoption; however, not so many answers to the question of where I'm from.

Check this out, it's really strange! Here, it says both my parents' names, and my date of birth is marked as "correct"...

but then over here, it says that my background is "unknown." My parents' names are missing and my date of birth "presumptive."

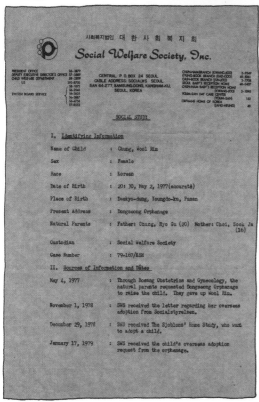

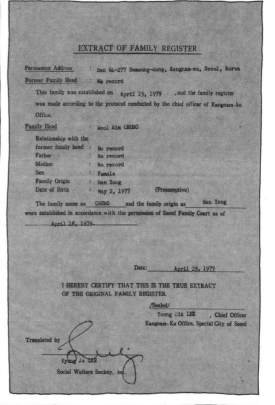

The fact that you can't trust what is in a Social Study is so commonplace that it's become a joke among adoptees.* Its contents are often made up, and descriptions of our appearances and personalities are almost identical in everybody's file. Even though it is the only link you have to your past, it's so untrustworthy that you become numb to it. I have stopped questioning and accepted this is how it is. It's a natural part of the narrative of being adopted.

But this is something else. These two documents have completely contradictory information about my parents.

I'll send SWS an e-mail and ask them to explain!

While you're at it, ask them if they know anything about this Mr. Jung. There is a strong possibility that he met your Korean parents when they gave you up.

I also check for answers online. Before long, I come across the expression "orphan hojuk."*

...orea, an orphan hojuk must be created in order to expedite adoptions. What you can see here is how an adoption that appears to be perfectly legal may be in reality based upon falsified information and fabricated papers, created by the adoption agency and governmental institutions working together.

And I learn that the term "orphan" isn't quite what you would think.*

UNICEF and global partners define an orphan as a child who has lost one or both parents. By this definition there were over 132 million orphans in sub-Saharan Africa, Asia, Latin America, and the Caribbean in 2005. This large figure represents not only children who have lost both parents, but also those who have lost a father but have a surviving mother or have lost their mother but have a surviving

I write to two adoption experts, one in Korea and one in Sweden, to see if they can tell me anything.

I'm in the process of going through my own adoption paperwork and have two different documents from Social Welfare Society. One was issued in 1978 and states the names of both of my parents. But the other is an excerpt from my family register, issued in 1979, and it says that there's no information about my background. In it I am stated as "head of family," and have the status "orphan." Do you know anything about this?

Thank you,
Lisa

Hi Lisa,

Seems that they lied in order to make you adoptable.
-J

If I may be blunt, your background/identity may have been manipulated, and your adoption was most likely arranged in an old-fashioned, patriarchal way, which is not legal.
-T

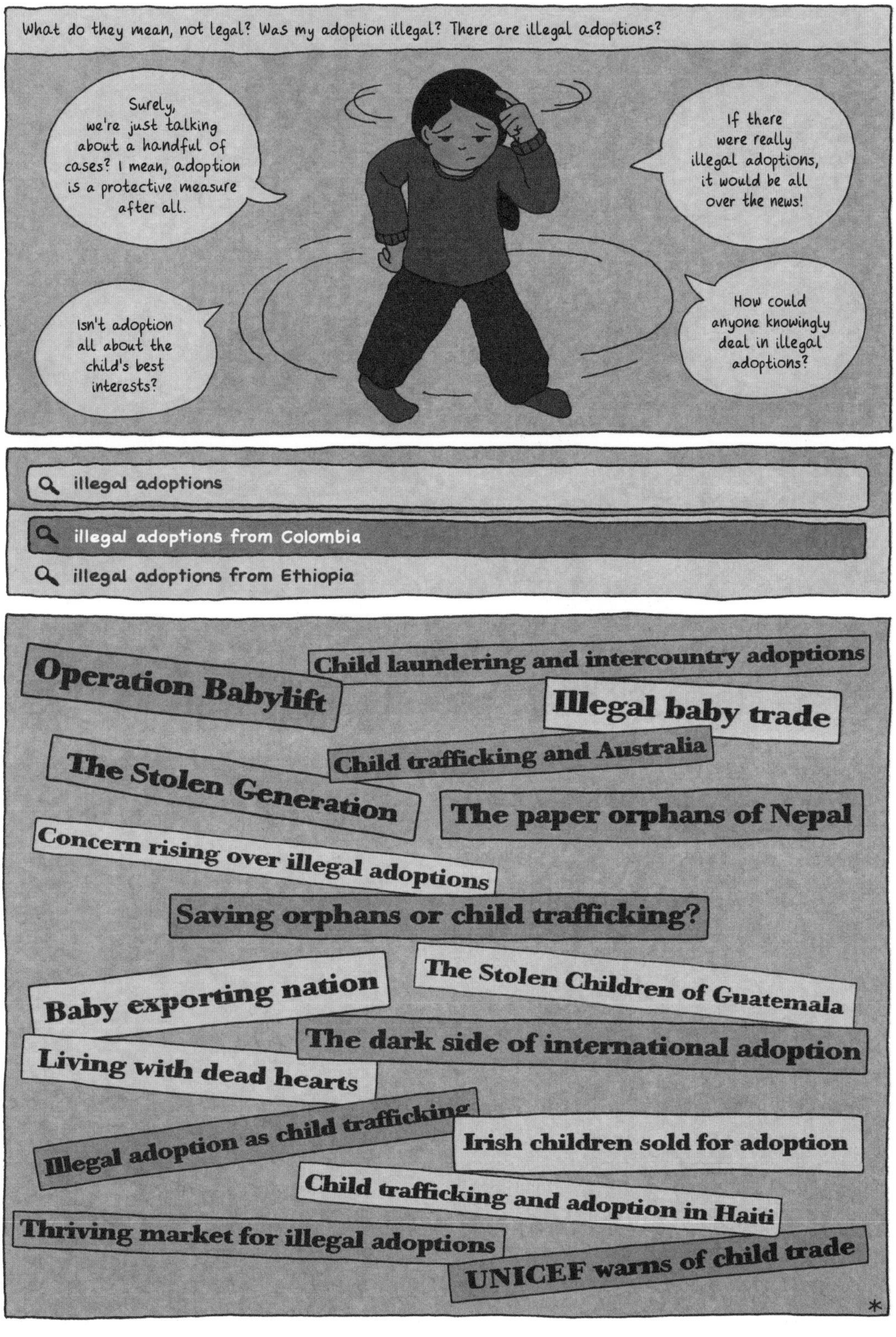
What do they mean, not legal? Was my adoption illegal? There are illegal adoptions?
Surely, we're just talking about a handful of cases? I mean, adoption is a protective measure after all.
If there were really illegal adoptions, it would be all over the news!
Isn't adoption all about the child's best interests?
How could anyone knowingly deal in illegal adoptions?
illegal adoptions
illegal adoptions from Colombia
illegal adoptions from Ethiopia
Operation Babylift
Child laundering and intercountry adoptions
Illegal baby trade
Child trafficking and Australia
The Stolen Generation
The paper orphans of Nepal
Concern rising over illegal adoptions
Saving orphans or child trafficking?
Baby exporting nation
The Stolen Children of Guatemala
The dark side of international adoption
Living with dead hearts
Illegal adoption as child trafficking
Irish children sold for adoption
Child trafficking and adoption in Haiti
Thriving market for illegal adoptions
UNICEF warns of child trade
*

International adoption was established as the practice we know today after the Korean War. Children are moved from the global South to the political West, where they are placed in white families, renamed, and have their mother tongue replaced. The demand for adoptable children outgrew the supply. Adoption became more about childless adults who wish to create a family, than orphans in need of protection. As large sums of money are involved, there's a strong incentive to illegally supply the market with what it needs: adoptable children, as young as possible.

Single mothers are hidden away in homes for unwed mothers, often run by adoption agencies, where they are advised to give up their babies for a better future. The women are cared for, but are thrown out if they dare choose to keep their children.

Parents are tricked into signing deals that they may not be able to understand, or even read. They're duped into believing that adoption means regular contact with their child, or told that the child is going to study in another city and later return home. Many spend years looking for their lost children.*

Of course, there are kidnappings. Children are snatched on the street and sold at orphanages where they're labeled as abandoned.*

Not to mention those who lost their children because other family members handed them over to an orphanage while the parents were at work.*

The children are supplied with documents claiming that they're orphans—laundered like money and transformed into legal "paper orphans." With the adoption comes a fabricated background story that the children were anonymously abandoned, maybe found on the steps of a church, at a police station, or outside a hospital.* Or there's an emotional story about a loving single mother with no choice in a patriarchal world, and who made the ultimate unselfish sacrifice a woman can make: giving up her child so they can have a better life. One could easily assume that the global South is overflowing with parents voluntarily abandoning their children.

So why do I have this orphan status? What happened during my adoption?

On this paper it says that the excerpt from the family register plays a part in the decision by Swedish authorities on an adoption, along with two other reports.

This means your adoption could be based on a document with false information!

That's crazy!

While we wait for answers from SWS, I'll try investigating on my own.

I'll write to some different institutions. Someone's got to know something about your orphanage.

If I'm lucky, I'll find someone who speaks English and can help us!

Richey googles the addresses he finds in my Social Study, but he keeps coming back to a place in Busan which seems to be the City Hall.

City Hall 시청역

When I search for the address of the hospital I only end up at City Hall. I wonder if the hospital used to be at that address.

I start telling people that I'm looking for my Korean parents.

...I've sent some inquiries to Korea. So now I'll just have to wait and see what happens.

I get mixed reactions.

But Lisa, why are you doing this? Do you really think it's going to make you any happier?

That's not why I'm doing it! I have questions about where I'm from and I want to try again to get some answers!

For my own sake and for the children's!

Some of my friends wonder how my adoptive parents feel about my search.

Don't you think it's difficult for your parents that you're doing this?

It annoys me that people impose guilt on me for asking questions about my roots.

Why would they have a problem with it? If you adopt, you should accept that your children will eventually want to know where they came from.

Everybody asks questions about where they come from. Why is it so controversial when adoptees do it?

No one questioned my dad or asked me how I felt when he traced his family history!

One thing that all of us root-searching adoptees know is that we're racing against the clock. With every passing day, our chances of a reunion become smaller. Every time we find out that an institution has closed down, it feels like another dead end and we blame ourselves for not starting sooner.

I'm trying not to feel disappointed. I keep telling myself that I don't care if they find my parents or not. All I'm really looking for is information about my adoption.

A Korean report shows that between 1995 and 2005 almost 80,000 adoptees returned to Korea to search for their roots; less than 3% managed to reunite with their first families.*

During my search, I come in contact with other adoptees.

Wow! There are thousands of different groups!

I wish I had this when I was growing up!

I join several adoption forums and discussion groups.*

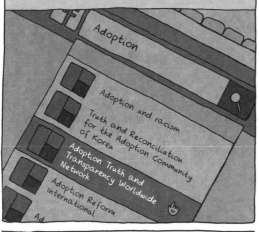

Adoption

Adoption and racism

Truth and Reconciliation for the Adoption Community of Korea

Adoption Truth and Transparency Worldwide Network

Adoption Reform International

Ad

The groups all have different themes and the members are adopted from many different countries, but there are many recurring stories.

Johanna Lundqvist*
11 hours ago

We have to fight against racism and how the adoption lobby treats us. The racism I encounter in adoption forums and from my own family is often harder to deal with than the racism I face in general. It's hard when you're not allowed to own your own story.

Show more

The ads are everywhere, adoptees searching for lost family members *

Searching for my birth mother

Searching for my father and sister

Searching for my birth parents

Looking for my siblings

Searching for my mother

Looking for my birth family

and parents searching for their lost children.*

Desperate birth mother searching for daughter

Birth father looking for my son

Searching for my younger sister

Birth parents looking for our son

Searching for my lost daughter

Birth family looking for our child

What if my parents are looking for me!

I've always pictured in my mind that they just gave us up, that it's an easy decision when you're penniless and desperate.

Listen to this, "The mothers didn't fully understand that the adoption meant a permanent separation. They still continued calling themselves mothers.

The mothers did not realize that international adoptions lead to loss of culture and language. They will never be able to communicate with their children even if reunited. Some parents were also pressured by their own family to give up their children! Most often by their own mothers!"*

It feels as if our parents are constantly being overlooked when discussing adoption. They're like footnotes, whose lives ceased existing the moment we're adopted.

Yeah, it's not often you hear about what it feels like to lose a child to adoption. Every adoption requires a family to be broken apart. Yet, you never hear about that grief.

It feels surreal to be part of this. To share experiences with these people I read about. To know that my own life is part of this messy, gruesome history.

I cautiously post in some critical adoption forums and quickly get some sympathy and validation. No one questions my feelings and opinions. Everyone is supportive and understanding. There are so many more of us than I thought.

I read many other stories on how their experiences are dismissed, taken, and reinterpreted, how "experts" who weren't adopted themselves, speak over them.

Adoptees recount how their criticisms are consistently being deleted from various adoption forums—forums that claim to be open to all adoptees, but in reality only allow positive perspectives.

Critical adoptees are brushed aside as angry, bitter, and ungrateful. Our yearnings for our original families and our pursuits for answers about severed biological ties are dismissed as only of interest to adoptees with mental issues, misfits, people who haven't "successfully" attached, people not capable of receiving the love offered to us.

How can a person's desire for their first family be seen as something hateful and pathological? How could it possibly be taboo?

What are you doing, Mom? Can we watch Pingu instead?

Sure!

I think about the letter Adoptionscentrum sent to me twenty years ago. They had a total lack of compassion and understanding as to why I was tracing my roots. They had the audacity to speculate about my background and indirectly tell me to stop searching for the mother I so desperately wanted to find.

"...chances are that Lisa's mother hadn't told anyone about Lisa's birth or adoption, and we can only hope that Lisa's mother today has a family, a husband, and children. A revelation of Lisa's existence would most likely break up that family and cause even more people pain.

I am convinced that Lisa's mother didn't have any other choice, either for herself or for Lisa, when she decided upon adoption. I'm also convinced that Lisa's mother has not forgotten her; it's just that we don't know where her mother is with her thoughts."

This reminds me of how scared I was when I first started my search as a teenager. I was terrified it would make my adoptive parents sad and they would view my search as a criticism of them.

Far too often, adoptees set their own feelings aside to show consideration of other people's thoughts and emotions about adoption.

We must not hurt our adoptive parents' feelings. Our questions can also offend other adoptees who don't feel the same way. And we also have to keep in mind our first families and protect them from ourselves.

Dear Lisa,

My name is Byeon Hee Sun and I am handling your case. You already have all the paperwork. The document called "Social Study" is the only one we have as well. With the aid of KAS (Korea Adoption Services), I will try to find your parents.

Since you weren't included in your family's register, our adoption agency was appointed your guardian. This is why your family register only contains information about you.

I tried to find the orphanage where you lived, to see if they have any more information about you, but I'm afraid it doesn't exist anymore. I'm terribly sorry about this.

I will try to find your foster mother. However, our file on her is very old, so the chances are slim.

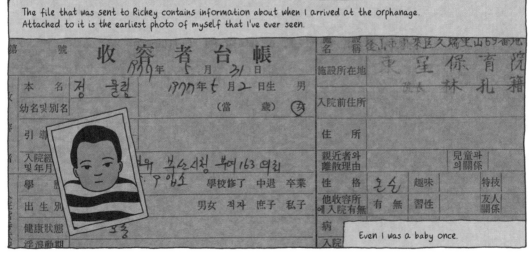

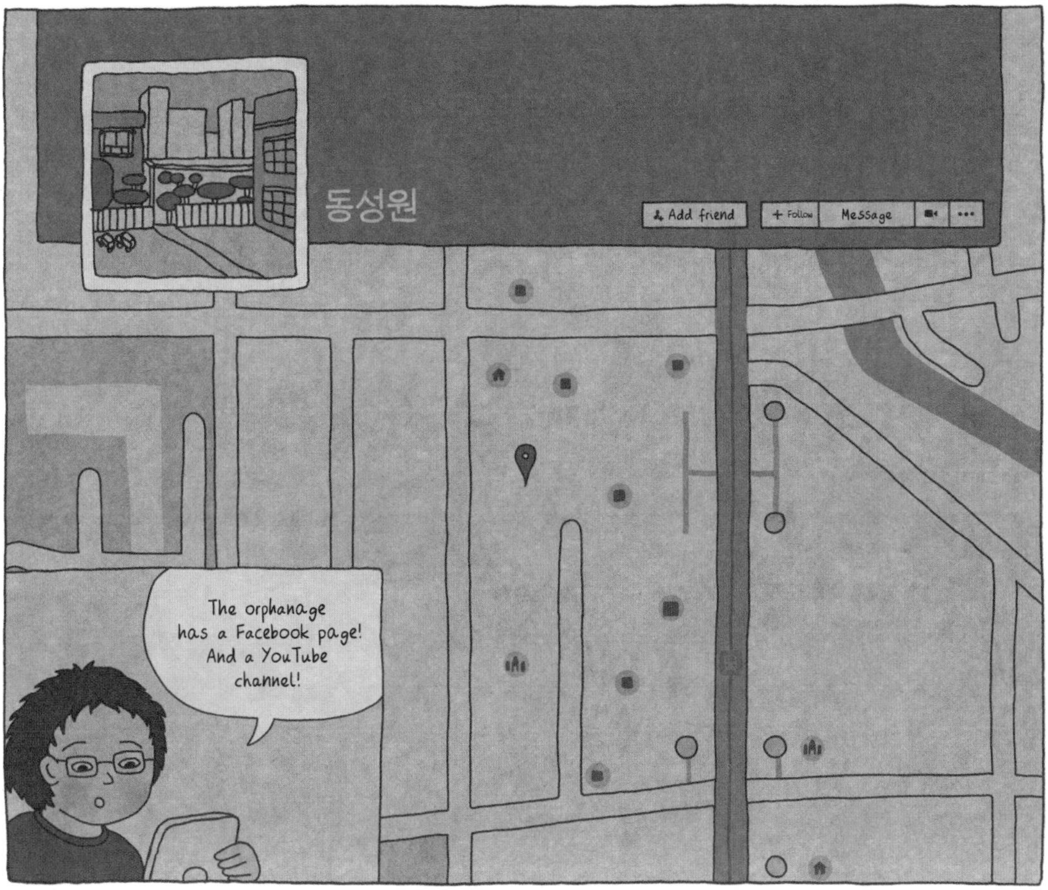
동성원
Add friend
+ Follow
Message
The orphanage has a Facebook page! And a YouTube channel!

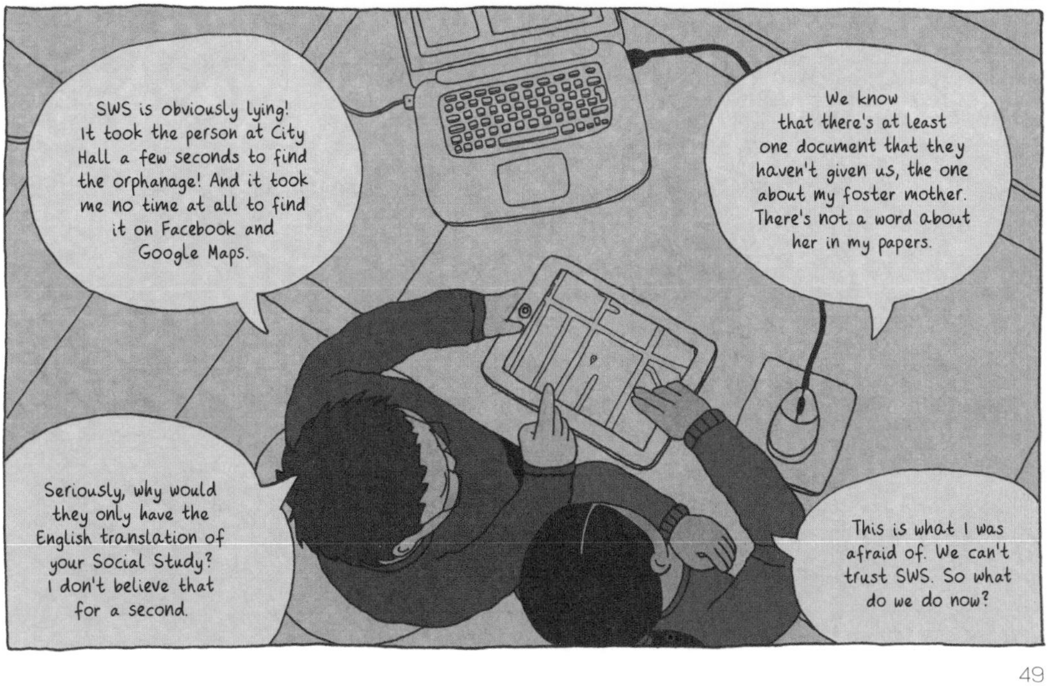
SWS is obviously lying! It took the person at City Hall a few seconds to find the orphanage! And it took me no time at all to find it on Facebook and Google Maps.
We know that there's at least one document that they haven't given us, the one about my foster mother. There's not a word about her in my papers.
Seriously, why would they only have the English translation of your Social Study? I don't believe that for a second.
This is what I was afraid of. We can't trust SWS. So what do we do now?

We decide to pretend we don't know what we know, and I send the following e-mail to SWS:

Dear Hee Sun, SWS,

Thank you for your e-mail. It's good to hear that you and KAS have begun to search for my family. I'm disappointed to hear about the birth hospital and the orphanage.

I wonder if you could tell me more about my foster mother? When did I stay with her? Where did she live?

My Social Study states that my relinquishment was arranged through "Bosang Obstetrics and Gynecology." Could you please share some information about this company?

I would once more like to request a copy of all records SWS has regarding my adoption, including those written in Korean. I noticed that there was no information on my foster mother, so there is one document that I'm missing.

Thank you for your help.

Best Regards,
Lisa

Dear Lisa,

Your birth hospital's name is Bosang Obstetrics and Gynecology, but it does not exist anymore.

I've attached all the adoption records that we have.

The Social Study was prepared before you moved in with your foster mother. That's why the adoption records didn't have any information about her. You stayed with her between May 2 and May 30, 1979. Your foster mother lived in Seoul and her name is Park Joon Ki.

Wow, talk about completely missing the point. She sent the same document that I already have.

Well, I have better news. A girl in my class is from Korea and she'd like to help us!

I showed her the file and e-mail from the orphanage, and she says that there's no information at all about your parents in it. And nothing about who left you at the orphanage.

Apparently you'd been to two other places before you arrived at the orphanage.

So this is what we know now—
I was born on May 2nd, 1977 at 8:30 PM, in a hospital nobody's heard of and no longer exists. After that, I was moved to two different places that no one knows about either, and when I was a week old I was sent to the orphanage. On May 2nd, 1979, I was moved to a foster mother in Seoul, whom I lived with for a month. On May 30th, 1979, I was put on a plane to Tokyo, and from Tokyo I flew to Sweden with an escort whose name we don't know. On June 3rd, 1979, I landed in Sweden. So we have information about my exact time of birth but no birth certificate that verifies it or proves I've even been born at all!

Look, another person at Busan City Hall replied. She's asking for authorization to send your case to the police, because they might be able to help us find your parents.

I'll send them everything we have. I hope they won't tell us that they have to go through adoption agencies, and refer us back to SWS.

As for me, I press on with my fruitless efforts to squeeze some answers out of SWS.

Thank you for your e-mail!

I apologize for bombarding you with so many questions, but when one has so little knowledge of one's past, everything becomes valuable.

I have some new questions:

1. Regarding the hospital, do you know what the address used to be?
2. Would it be possible to track down my foster mother? I would very much like to meet her.
3. Regarding the dates in my family register and Social Study, how come the Social Study says that my birth date is "accurate," and the hojuk says "presumptive"? Is there any reason to doubt whether I was born on May 2nd 1977? Also, is the date according to the lunar or the solar calendar?
4. Can I trust that the names of my parents are real?
5. Any updates on the search process?

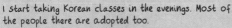

I start taking Korean classes in the evenings. Most of the people there are adopted too.

안녕하세요! 잘지내요!

It sucks that we don't get to study our first language for free. At the very least we should receive a grant for the course fees. Adoptive parents get 75,000 Kronor, for heaven's sake.*

Richey's classmate Min-Jeong and I meet, and I get the same jittery feeling as I did when the Koreans visited my village in the eighties.

I wonder what it feels like to be a real Korean...

I ask a thousand stupid questions about Korea, and I feel like a dumb Westerner.

What do you eat besides kimchi and bulgogi?

Do people in Korea know how many kids have been sent for adoption?

Min-Jeong helps us read my papers.

Thanks for helping me with this.

I feel pretty lonely here in Sweden. I'm just like a stupid foreigner.

I think this is the reason why I came here to study.

We were fated to meet, so that I could help you with your search. This way, my Korean language can be of use!

A few days after Richey's e-mail to the police, we notice that they're searching for my parents on Facebook.

Wow, that was fast. Now you're famous in Busan!

I really hope that my parents see this.

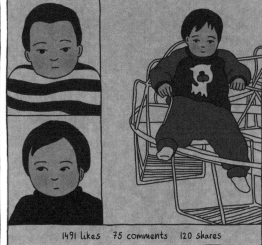

1491 likes   75 comments   120 shares

Dear Lisa,

1. Your birth hospital's address is Daekyo-dong, Yeongdo-gu, Busan.
2. I'll review the old records of your foster mother and try to reach her. Hopefully, she still has the same contact information. I'll let you know when I have any news.
3. We got the information about your birth parents from the orphanage, so the Social Study was written based on this information, under the belief that it is correct. However, our agency didn't meet with your birth parents in person. This is why SWS registered your birth date on your hojuk with the note that it could be presumptive.
4. All the information was given to our agency through the orphanage, so I hope that your birth parents left the correct information at the orphanage at that time.
5. As I told you before, you already have all the information. I forwarded all the documents to KAS. I'll get back to you as soon as I have any news from them.

Dear Hee Sun, SWS,

Thank you for replying so quickly to my last e-mail; your answers were very helpful, and much appreciated. I'm a bit concerned about the lack of information that SWS has on file about me and my adoption. Is there really nothing more?

Here is a list of the documents that I hope to find:

1. The original Korean version of my Social Study. The one I have states that it is a translation.
2. The records of my foster family placement.
3. A record of my birth.
4. The form that my parents signed when they handed me over to the orphanage.
5. Any correspondence regarding my adoption. For example, it says that an institution named "Busan Children's Guidance Clinic" was involved. Do you know anything more about that?

A week later, I receive my last e-mail from SWS.

As I told you before, you already have all the available documents.

Regarding "Busan Children's Guidance Clinic," we don't have any information. The place ceased to exist a long time ago and there is no information about it. Therefore, I am unable to explain what kind of role it played in your adoption process.

Lastly, as to searching for your birth parents, I recently heard from KAS that they unfortunately have failed to find your birth parents. They checked several potential people, but none even partially matched the information we have on your birth parents. Due to the lack of information, it is very difficult to search for your birth parents. I regret to say that this is all I can provide.

I'd like to tell you that there is another method: using mass media. In Korea, there is a TV show called "I Miss That Person," where people look for missing family members, including adoptees. If you are interested in this show, please let me know, and I'll help you.

-Byeon Hee Sun, SWS

I'm hurled twenty years back in time.

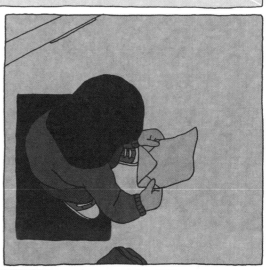

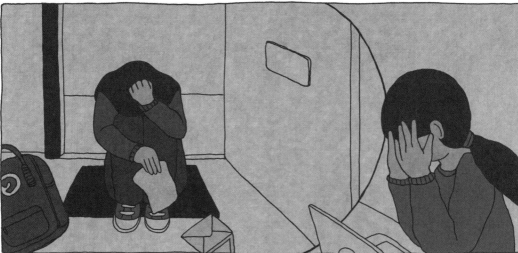

Back then, when I embarked on my first search, I believed my adoption was proof that I was never supposed to exist.

I'd grown up with the feeling that I was a mistake. Who gives up a wanted child?

These emotions were difficult to process. The people I confided in tended to translate my thoughts into their versions of my life. The only thing that belonged to me was my wish for death. I wanted the intense yearning for my roots to vanish like magic. It only resulted with me locked up in a psychiatric ward.

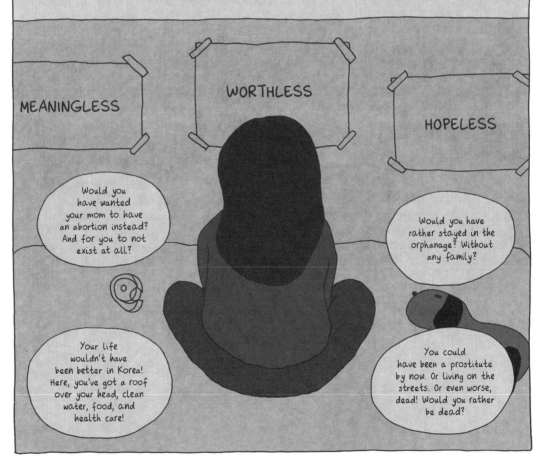

MEANINGLESS

WORTHLESS

HOPELESS

Would you have wanted your mom to have an abortion instead? And for you to not exist at all?

Would you have rather stayed in the orphanage? Without any family?

Your life wouldn't have been better in Korea! Here, you've got a roof over your head, clean water, food, and health care!

You could have been a prostitute by now. Or living on the streets. Or even worse, dead! Would you rather be dead?

I didn't stop looking for answers, despite all the medication and therapy and my countless attempts to change.

Over the years, I wrote hundreds of letters to my parents, most of them to my mother. And piles and piles of awful poetry.

The few times I saw other Asians, I looked to see if we had any common features. What if it was my mother who was looking for me!

For a while I tried to find God.

In God's family, we're all adopted children. He loves us all like his own. In God's eyes, there are no unwanted children. We're all special.

I really wanted to believe this, that there was a higher purpose to my existence, that no one is here by mistake.

But it didn't work.

In the end, it's how you feel inside that counts. It doesn't matter what you try to convince yourself. The pain and the yearning are a part of you. If you can't manage to die, you simply have to figure out a way to live.

Dear Hee Sun, SWS,

My name is Richard Wyver and from now on, I'll be taking over the correspondence relating to Lisa's birth family search. To begin with, I'd like to state that I understand fully that it is within SWS's interests to conceal records and cover up mistakes made in the past. However, I'd like to remind you that you are dealing with real people's lives here: while SWS cannot repair the damage caused and the lives shattered by the adoption industry, you can treat adult adoptees with respect, and allow them to find out the truth about their early years, even if it may be painful, or may cast your company in a negative light.

Lisa has made several requests for information and copies of documents that you have on file. You have repeatedly refused to hand over documents that she is legally entitled to see. You have told Lisa a number of times that the only documents SWS has are the same as hers. We are well aware that this is untrue. For starters, you have information about a foster family—why have you not sent papers containing this to Lisa? You also claimed that SWS only has a copy of the English translation of the Social Study—this is absolutely unbelievable. It is inconceivable that SWS would dispose of a document written in Korean and keep a poor translation of it instead.

So now I demand that you send me a full copy of Lisa's file. I would like every piece of information you have on her, regardless of whether you think it is irrelevant. I am not interested in inaccurate translations: I want copies of the original Korean documents. If you are unable to send this, please direct me to who I need to contact in order to access them.

I would also appreciate it if you could e-mail exactly what SWS has done so far in their search for Lisa's roots, so we can decide how to continue with it. I would like to know what facts about her past have actually been established, and if SWS has recorded false information or created fake documents for her, and why this may have been done.

We are well aware that Lisa's true story may be unpleasant. Your reluctance to hand over information, your previous insistence that the orphanage had closed down (we knew it hadn't. They do have a record of Lisa being there too; they sent it to me a few weeks ago), your reluctance to pass on information about "Busan Children's Guidance Clinic," and the fact that Lisa's adoption was arranged privately (from the Swedish end), all indicate that there was illegal activity involved. As I mentioned above, I understand that SWS would want to cover this up. However, I can assure you that Lisa is prepared for the truth, whatever it may be, and that we won't judge you for it.

-Richey

Dear Richey,

As I explained before, SWS does not have the Korean version of the Social Study. At the time of Lisa's adoption, many documents were simply not filed. There is no reason for SWS to hide or conceal any documents. Since many of the cases from the sixties and seventies have insufficient information, this can lead to extreme difficulty in finding the birth family.

I asked the orphanage to give me all the information about Lisa. I also asked if anyone there knew anything about Busan Children's Guidance Clinic, but they replied that they don't have any information on it. Again, I have given all the answers I have, based on information about Lisa that we have.

I'm attaching a file that is a summary of Lisa's adoption process.

Richey also writes to KAS, who have been notably absent during this whole process, except for a short e-mail to verify that they're looking for my parents together with SWS. Unlike when I wrote to them, he receives an answer immediately.

Dear Richey,

First of all, I am very, very sorry about this late reply. We've talked to SWS and they said that the Korean version of your Social Study does not exist. At the time around the sixties and seventies there were no regulations set up regarding preserving documents. I've seen many cases where there isn't enough information. But we've seen Korean original documents and compared them to their English translations, and they're usually correctly translated.

We haven't heard of "Busan Children's Guidance Clinic" either. We think it might have been a temporary protection center governed by Busan city. But we did find information about something called "Busan Total Child Protection Center." They think the Busan Children's Guidance Clinic used to provide counseling services. They themselves provide temporary protection services since 1987. I'm attaching their contact information. I also contacted Lisa's orphanage, and they said they have the child card that was written at the time when she was admitted. We've sent an official request for this paper. Once I receive it, I will let you know. I'm really sorry about not giving you clear answers to all your queries.

Sincerely,
Kong Mi Na, KAS

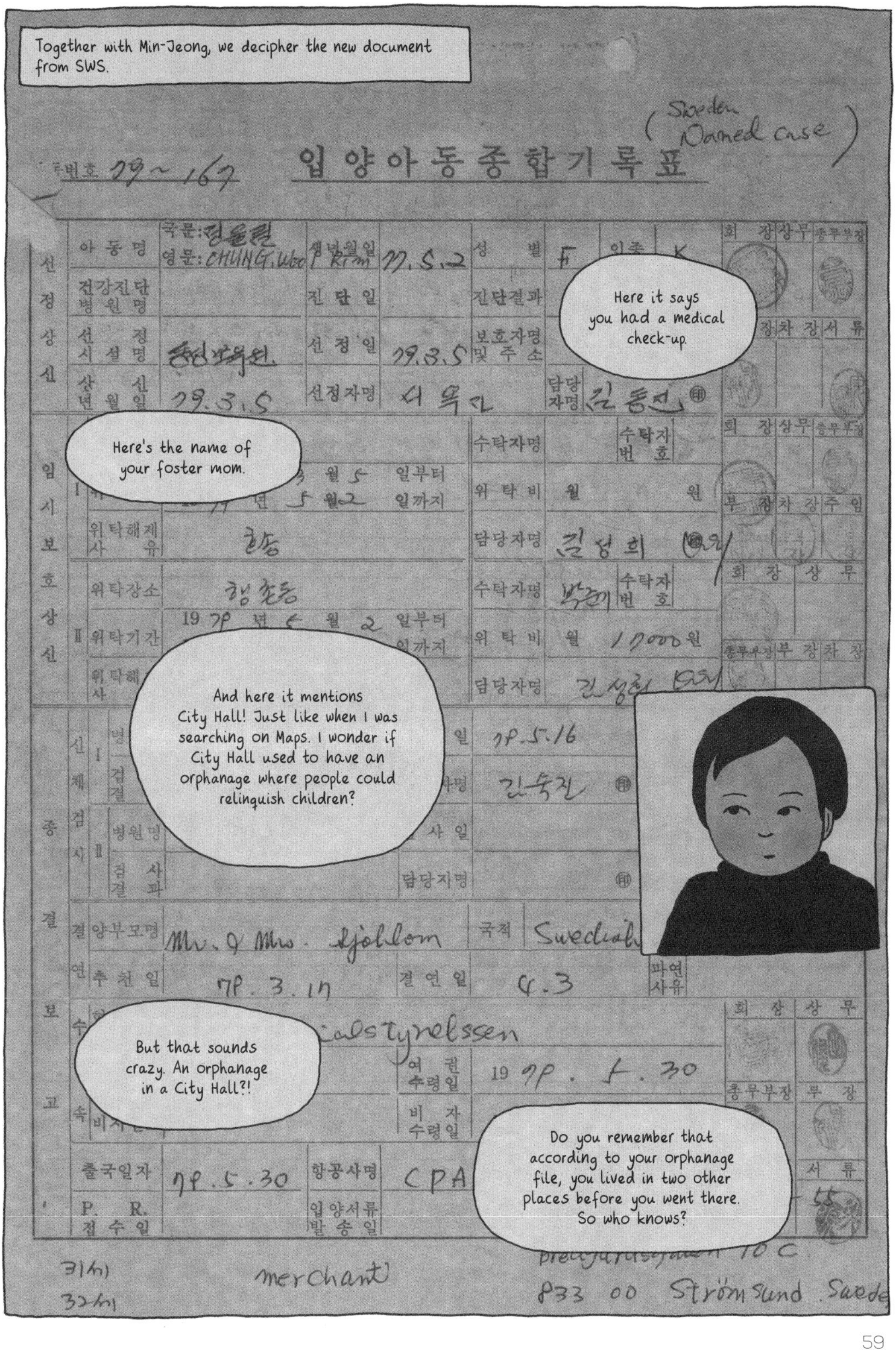
Together with Min-Jeong, we decipher the new document from SWS.
Sweden Named case
입양아동종합기록표
Here it says you had a medical check-up.
Here's the name of your foster mom.
And here it mentions City Hall! Just like when I was searching on Maps. I wonder if City Hall used to have an orphanage where people could relinquish children?
But that sounds crazy. An orphanage in a City Hall?!
Do you remember that according to your orphanage file, you lived in two other places before you went there. So who knows?

Dear Hee Sun, SWS,

Thank you for your reply and for the document. I appreciate your honesty regarding the non-filing of Korean records, and I understand that it must make your job very challenging when it comes to family-searching. However, I think that you can agree that it appears a little strange that SWS would keep a paper with Lisa's natural parents' and grandparents' names in English, but dispose of all records that have their names in Korean. It is necessary for us to collect as many documents relating to Lisa as possible, so if you do come across anything else in your research, I would be very grateful if you could send it to me, even if it doesn't seem to be important, or contain new information.

I'm attaching a copy of the file the orphanage sent me. I wonder if you could have a look at it, and see what you make of it. You'll see that it doesn't have the parents' names on it. It shows that Lisa entered the orphanage on May 9th but before that she was at "City Hall" and "Children's Welfare Clinic." Do you think that this means her parents relinquished her to the City Hall or the Children's Welfare Clinic, rather than directly to the orphanage? Perhaps this would explain the lack of information about Lisa's parents that the orphanage had. I would be really interested to know your opinion on this! I wonder if this clinic still exists or if Busan City Hall has records of Lisa being there? I have a contact in Busan Council that I will write to and ask, but I would appreciate it if you could look into this too.

The fact that the orphanage file doesn't contain the parents' names, and the fact that the parents' names don't appear on any other documents raises some interesting questions that I'd like to ask you now. I believe that, given the nature of your job, you are probably better qualified to answer these questions than anyone else, and I would really appreciate it if you could give me your sincere, honest answers:

1. I understand that the Social Study is primarily intended for the adoptive parents. It is well known among Korean adoptees that the information about the child in the Social Study is the same (or very similar) for each adoptee. Of the adoptees we know personally and of the adoptees we have read about, not a single one has seen a Korean Social Study. Is it possible then, in your opinion, that there never was a Korean Social Study for Lisa?

2. If this is the case, in your experience of adoption records and with your knowledge of the adoption process in the 1970s, do you think it is possible that the information about Lisa's parents and her background story could have been fabricated?

3. Do you, personally, feel that the names stated are correct?

Lisa and I both realize that it is unlikely that we will ever find her parents. However, we are absolutely determined to find out as much of her history as we can, not only for Lisa herself, but also for our two children. They are very young now, but when they start asking questions about their heritage, questioning why they look different compared to other children at school, and wanting to know who their grandparents were, we want to be able to tell them something. We want them to be able to grow up feeling proud of their Korean heritage.

-Richey

Hello Kong Mi Na, KAS

Thank you for getting back to us. It's good to know that you have begun your investigations. We're looking forward to seeing the document from the orphanage; perhaps it will give us some more clues. May I ask you a small favor? While you are in contact with the orphanage, could you please ask if they know anyone who worked there in 1977-1979 that we might be able to contact? It would be fantastic to find someone who may have known Lisa as a baby; we may find someone who remembers her background story.

I suppose that if Lisa was handed in at City Hall or to the children's clinic, then one of these places may have some record of her being left there. I imagine that her parents must have had to sign a legal form confirming that they wanted to leave their baby in the care of Busan City. Could you please try to contact Busan City to see if anyone there could help us find any record of Lisa being there? Her Social Study suggests that her name, Wool Rim, was given to her by the orphanage, but they may be able to locate records of her from her parents' names. Thank you!

We managed to procure another file from SWS: the summary of Lisa's adoption. I have attached it, just in case you don't have a copy. We're very keen to find out about some of the people named on this document. I wonder if you could see if you could find out more information about them. Thank you very much for your help!

-Richey

The document from SWS is pretty blotchy, so I magnify it to get a closer look.

Richey!
You're not going to believe this I zoomed in on the document to clean it up...

and there's a back side! If you flip the image you can see that there's text on the other side!

Richey immediately writes to SWS. They send us the reverse side and we see a name we recognize.

So all this time they've denied all knowledge of this place and Mr. Jung, yet all along his name was on a document of theirs! I wonder how much more information they're doing their best to keep from us.

And KAS has sent me the document from the orphanage. It's the one that we already have, of course. Seriously!

Listen, I just realized something. I can't believe I didn't think of this before. You were handed over to an institution run by the City of Busan, the local government. So in that case, there's bound to be some sort of city archive there where they would register children who became wards of the state. And where else would they keep this but City Hall! Maybe that's why I ended up at "City Hall" when I was searching on Google.

I thought it was a mistake, or that your hospital used to be at the same address. What if that address isn't about the place where you were born or stayed, but is the place where your relinquishment and care arrangements were organized. "City Hall" isn't the City Hall as a physical place with an orphanage, hospital, or whatever, but it's City Hall, the institution— the local authority responsible for the citizens of Busan. I'll e-mail them now!

We receive an answer almost immediately. There are documents about me at City Hall!

But they've sent everything to KAS.

Yeah, now we'll never see them.

Hello Mi Na, KAS!

I contacted Busan City myself, and they've found a document about Lisa's relinquishment! They say that they have emailed this document to you, rather than directly to us. Please, please, please could you contact me as soon as you get the document! And please could you forward it to me!

Best regards,
- Richey

Hello Richey,

I received the documents from Busan City Hall.

However, I cannot release them for now since I haven't gotten Lisa's birth mother's consent yet. I hope Lisa can understand this.

Sincerely,
Mi Na, KAS

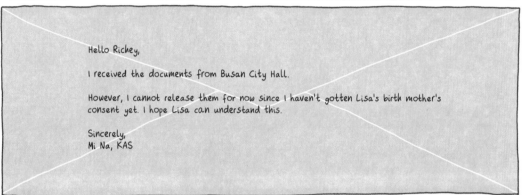

Hello! This is completely unacceptable! I want you to send me every document right now! And if there's anything classified in there, can't you just black it out?...Why does Lisa's mother have to give her approval?

...so that means there is information about Lisa's family in the documents! But if we don't find Lisa's mother, you can't do anything else?

...but the other information? Surely you can let us see that? This is about Lisa's life, it might be the only information there is about her.

I finally learn the reason for my adoption. And it reminds me of one of the possible scenarios that I've fantasized about over the years—complicated teen romance. I also find out that someone gave me my name before I came to the orphanage.

Min-Jeong translates and tells me:

Your parents were members of the same club within the Catholic Church and had known each other since they were fourteen. One night there was a going-away party for one of the club's members, who was off to do his military service. Your mother was sixteen. When the party was over it was late, and she spent the night with your dad. She didn't realize until four months later that she was pregnant. Since abortion was against her religious beliefs, she kept you. She kept her pregnancy a secret until she was eight months pregnant. Your father was informed but there was nothing he could do. They were very young and still students, so given their circumstances it was impossible for them to take care of you. They thought it would be better to give the baby up for adoption.

This sounds like an American high school movie— teenagers, a party, and an unwanted baby.

She kept me a secret until she was eight months pregnant. Sounds like she actually wanted to keep me.

Do you agree that there are, sort of, too many details? It's pretty intimate. I mean, why did they have to tell the whole story of why my Omma spent the night with my father?

I think we should take this with a grain of salt. Only someone with something to hide would give this much information in this situation.

I go to bed that night with a strange feeling in my body.

It feels like something has ended. My hopes have died. This is probably all I'm going to get.

Good night, sweetie.

It's time to move on.

LISA!!!

MRS. KIM E-MAILED! THE POLICE FOUND YOUR MOTHER!!!

YOU CAN FINALLY FIND OUT WHERE YOU'RE FROM!

PART 3 **Scriptio Inferior**

Hello Hee Sun, SWS,

Two weeks ago I contacted Busan City Hall to ask if they've kept records about adopted children. They replied that yes, they did—and better still, they were able to find a file on Lisa at once! The file contained several documents, naming her parents, stating their dates of birth and reasons for abandonment. Busan City couldn't send the file to us directly, and sent it to KAS instead. KAS refused to hand over the file to us, and it seemed that all hope was lost.

Then, last Tuesday, quite out of the blue, Busan Police contacted me: they had found Lisa's mother. They've spent the last month contacting everyone with the mother's name and of a similar age in Busan—the 70th person they contacted was Lisa's mother.

Lisa hasn't had direct contact with her mother yet, as we're waiting to hear what she and the police feel is the best step to take next. It must have been a huge shock to her, to hear that her daughter was looking for her after all these years. We really hope she has someone she can talk to, and access to support and advice. If you have any suggestions what would be a good procedure to follow in preparation for a reunion, please do let me know.

In addition to our good news, there is one negative thing I would like to bring to your attention. I have not been satisfied with the role that KAS played in the searching process. A few weeks ago you wrote the following to Lisa: "I recently heard from KAS that they unfortunately have failed in searching for your birth parents. They checked several possible people, but no one even partially matches the information we have on your birth parents. For now, due to lack of information, it is very difficult to search for your birth parents." I'm not sure the information that KAS gave you was correct; in fact, I'm not sure they tried to search for Lisa's parents at all. The police told us that the difficulty they had was caused by the fact that there were so many people with similar names and details (120 people with Lisa's Mom's name and age living in Busan); whereas KAS told you that there was nobody who even partially matched the information we had on Lisa's parents.

It was, in the end, relatively easy to find Lisa's mother; she wasn't exactly hiding. As Lisa's mother had left complete, correct details about herself when she gave Lisa up, and these records were so easily accessible from Busan City Hall, it is very sad that KAS were not able to find her themselves.

With best regards,
Richey

I know I have to keep my emotions under control. After all, I don't know if they've found the right person. Only a DNA test can show if we're really mother and daughter.

I wonder what makes the police so sure it's my mother. I wish they could tell me a little more!

And they've sent me a photo of her!!!

They write that my mother needs more time before we can get in touch.

The photo I've been waiting for all my life.

We look a little bit alike, don't we? Or maybe not?

A few months later there's suddenly a phone call from Korea.

Hello? Is this Lisa? I'm calling from Busan Police. Your mother would like to speak to you in a bit.

Min-Jeong! Come on, answer the phone! Wake up!

Min-Jeong! Hi! It's Lisa! Can I come over? My mother's about to call!

I'm going to need an interpreter!

Good luck! Hope it goes well.

Don't forget to ask some questions that could verify whether she's the right person!

I rush to the bus to go to Min-Jeong's place. I feel so unprepared.

What on earth am I going to say? What do you say to a mother you've never spoken to before?

The call I've been waiting for all my life. I've dreamed about it so often that the images of us talking have almost become real. I'll finally be able to hear my mother's voice.

How do you feel? Are you okay?

Yeah
Well

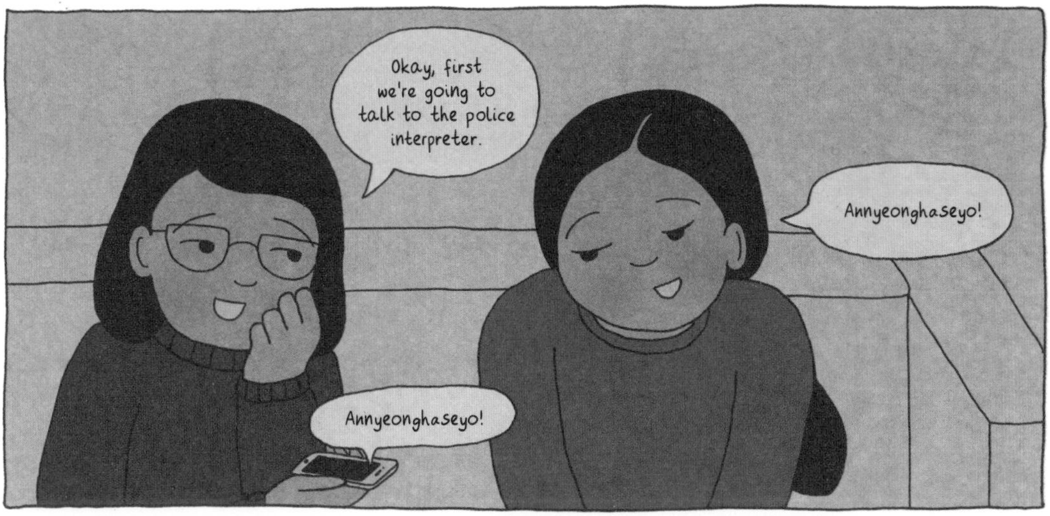
Okay, first we're going to talk to the police interpreter.
Annyeonghaseyo!
Annyeonghaseyo!

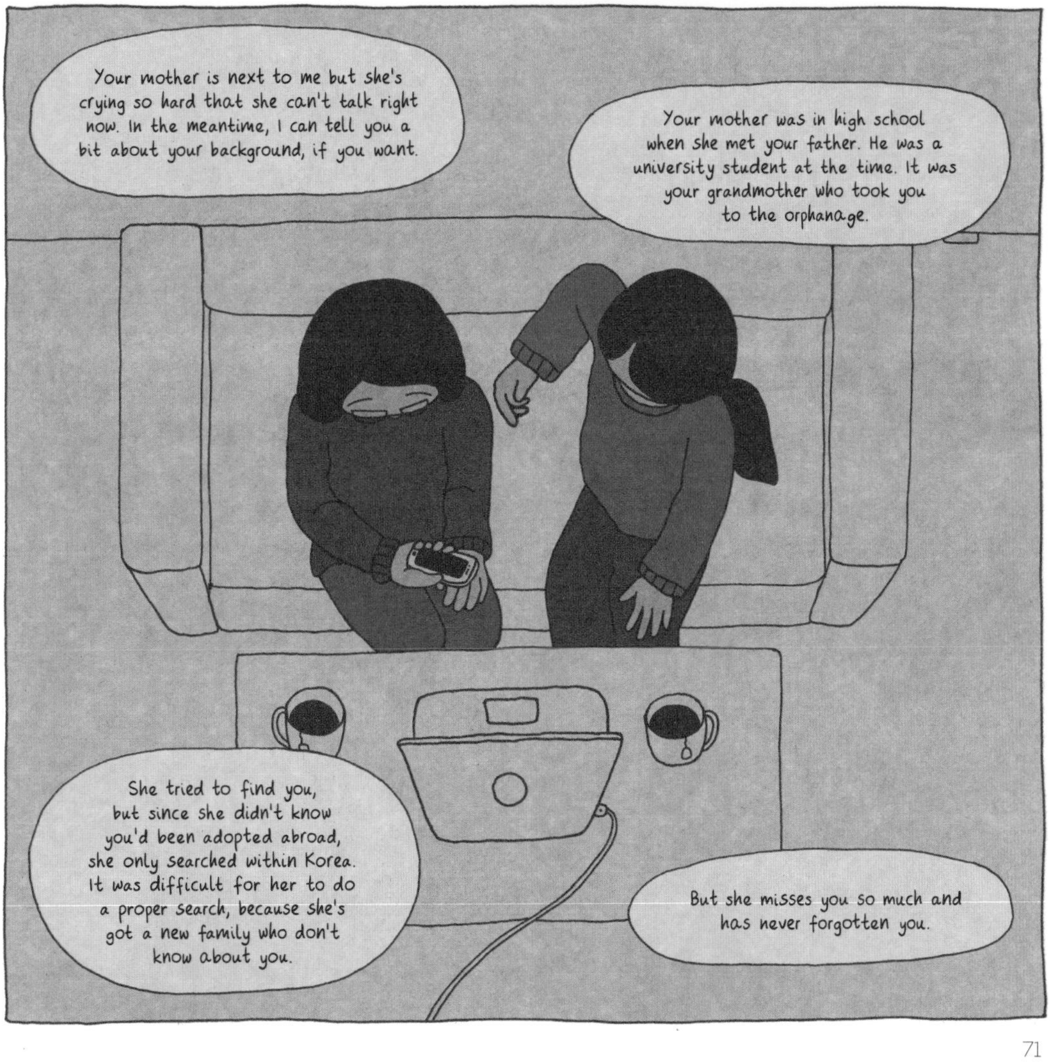
Your mother is next to me but she's crying so hard that she can't talk right now. In the meantime, I can tell you a bit about your background, if you want.
Your mother was in high school when she met your father. He was a university student at the time. It was your grandmother who took you to the orphanage.
She tried to find you, but since she didn't know you'd been adopted abroad, she only searched within Korea. It was difficult for her to do a proper search, because she's got a new family who don't know about you.
But she misses you so much and has never forgotten you.

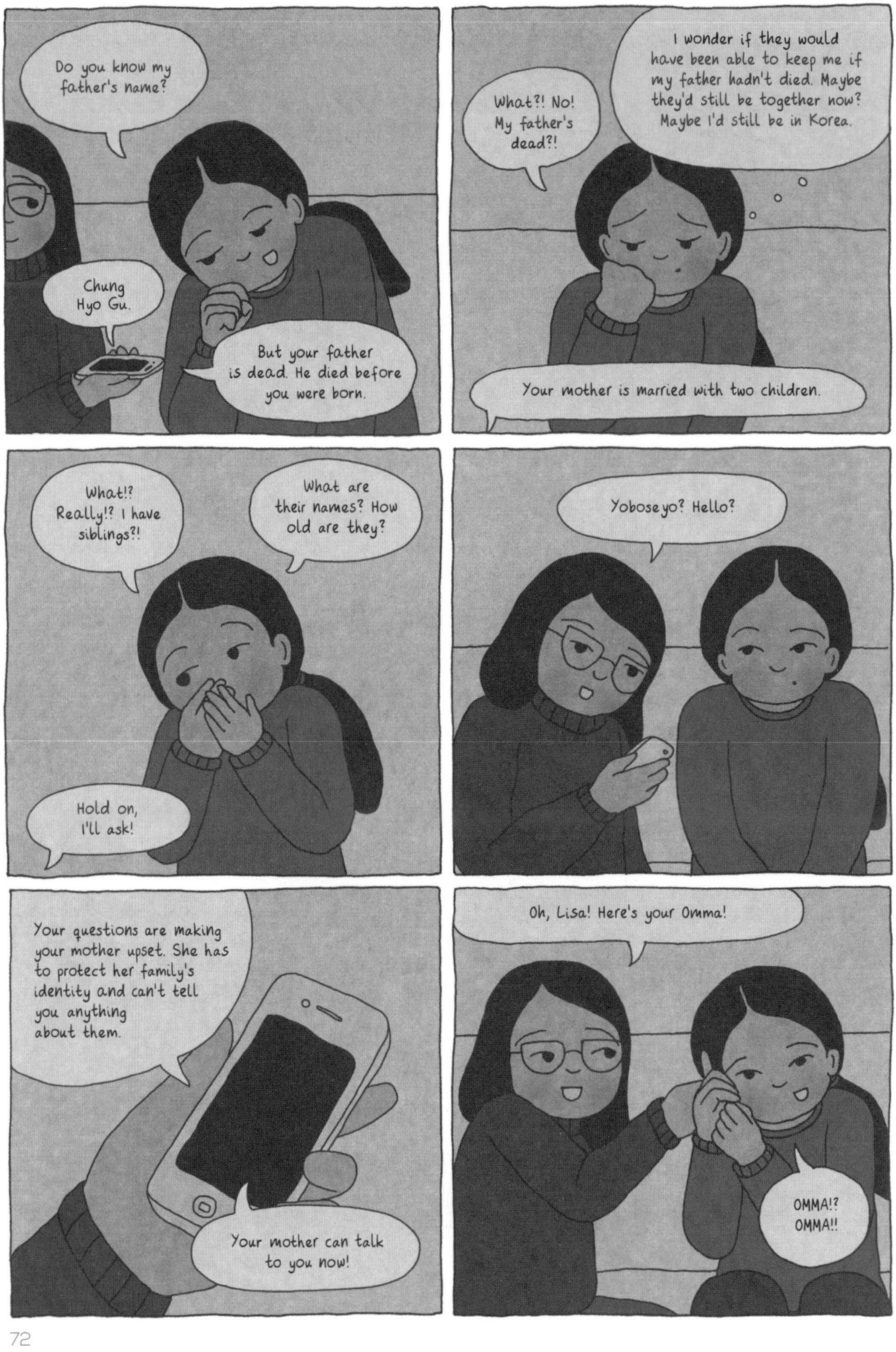
Do you know my father's name?
Chung Hyo Gu.
But your father is dead. He died before you were born.
What?! No! My father's dead?!
I wonder if they would have been able to keep me if my father hadn't died. Maybe they'd still be together now? Maybe I'd still be in Korea.
Your mother is married with two children.
What!? Really!? I have siblings?!
What are their names? How old are they?
Hold on, I'll ask!
Yoboseyo? Hello?
Your questions are making your mother upset. She has to protect her family's identity and can't tell you anything about them.
Your mother can talk to you now!
Oh, Lisa! Here's your Omma!
OMMA!? OMMA!!

The first thing my Omma said to me was my Korean name, Wool Rim. "Oolim," she says, and I realize that I —and everyone I know—have been pronouncing it wrongly all my life. Hearing my Omma's sobbing voice saying "Oolim" over and over again, I start liking it. I was always a bit embarrassed about it and thought it sounded harsh and ugly. But "Oolim" is soft, and the pronunciation fits its poetic meaning: "forest echo." I have the most beautiful name in the world.

Omma, I've been thinking about you all my life! And I've been looking for you for almost twenty years!

I'm so happy I finally found you! I didn't think it would ever happen!

Omma! I don't know what to say... There's so much I want to say! Where should I begin? Oh, right, you're a grandma! You've got two grand-kids! A three-year-old and a one-year-old.

Wool Rim, your grandmother died a few years ago. Just before she passed away she told me never to forget you, my first child. Over the years, when we've donated money, we've done it in your name.

It's an awkward phone call, and everything I say sounds like a cliché. I tell her about some organizations in Korea that can help with reunions, and ask her to look them up.

There's a place that runs English classes for reunited mothers, where you can be anonymous.

I promise to write! And I'll send pictures of your grandkids.

And there are loads of books by adoptees that I can recommend!

We're coming to Korea next year, so I hope we can meet then. Bye, Omma! Bye!

Min-Jeong obtains Mrs. Kim's e-mail address. We decide that she'll mediate between Omma and me, since I can't write directly to her.

What a strange conversation! I didn't know what to say at all, and she didn't say a lot either. Except that my dad is dead.

Lisa, this may be hard to accept, but you shouldn't believe everything that was said during that call.

I don't know if you noticed, but when you started asking questions about your mother's family, Mrs. Kim interrupted the interpreter. She told your mother that she shouldn't tell you anything personal.

Hi! How'd it go? How was it? What did she say?

My dad is dead! I'll never have the chance to meet him.

We have to visit his grave when we go to Korea. So I can say a proper goodbye.

My Dear Omma,

I can't believe that I've finally found you. It makes me so happy; words cannot express it. You've been in my thoughts for as long as I can remember. Over the years I've written you lots of letters and poems, telling you about myself and my life. I first started searching for you when I was seventeen. I asked my parents for my adoption papers and that's when I first learned your name. I asked my Korean adoption agency, Social Welfare Society, for help but was told that nothing could be done for me. I grieved for many years but moved on with my life, hoping that other forces would one day unite us. This summer, however, I decided to start searching again, but was again told by my agency that you could not to be found. I had given up all hope until the police in Busan sent me the message that they had found you.

Thirty-six years is a long time to be apart. There is so much I want to say, so much I want to tell you about. My hope is that we can reclaim some of the things we've lost, but most of all, move forward, and look to the future. I understand your need for privacy, and I understand that you may want and need to keep me and your family separate. The only thing I have ever wished for is to know that you are alive and safe, and for you to know that you are in my thoughts and in my heart.

I don't know anything about my beginnings, but let me tell you about what I do know. I stayed in an orphanage in Busan called Dongseong between May 9th 1977 and May 2nd 1979. In 1979 I was selected for adoption and was moved to Seoul to a foster mother called Park Joon Ki with whom I stayed for a month. On May 30th 1979 I was flown to Sweden in the company of an escort. On June 3rd I arrived in Stockholm, Sweden, where I was met by my adoptive parents and my brother, who is four years older and also adopted from Korea.

As you probably understand, I have a million questions for you, but I don't want to drown you with them. So here are just a few. Could you tell me more about having me? Who were you then? How was your pregnancy? In Sweden, when you're expecting a baby, everybody says that you should ask your mother about her delivery, since they are passed on from mother to daughter! And could you tell me something about my father? Who was he? What was he like? What did he look like? How did he die?

This letter could go on forever, but I'll stop now and tell you more in my next letter.

Your daughter

Not long after sending the letter to my Omma, I get an e-mail in Korean from the policewoman, Mrs. Kim.

I think I've got a reply from Omma!

She's sent a scanned letter and I think I can make out the words "Wool Rim" and "Omma."

I send the letter to Min-Jeong to translate, but she's on a trip somewhere, so things are delayed. I feel frustrated and sad that I can't communicate with my Omma without having to ask for help. Apart from my children, she's the only biological bond that I know of. Not only have we been separated, I've also lost my mother tongue. I'll never be able to fully tell her who I really am.

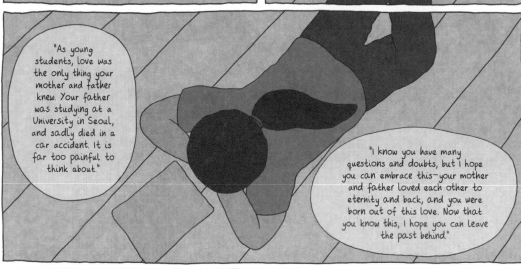

"As young students, love was the only thing your mother and father knew. Your father was studying at a University in Seoul, and sadly died in a car accident. It is far too painful to think about."

"I know you have many questions and doubts, but I hope you can embrace this—your mother and father loved each other to eternity and back, and you were born out of this love. Now that you know this, I hope you can leave the past behind."

I ask Min-Jeong to tell me more about the letter, about my Omma's handwriting and how she expresses herself. And whether she can read anything between the lines.

I think your mother is well-educated. She's eloquent and expresses herself in a cultured way.

Her language is very poetic and philosophical. I'd guess she's also deeply religious. And she's very Korean.

I've longed so much for that letter. But just like after the phone call, I just feel a big emptiness. Omma barely tells me anything about herself, nothing about me, and nothing about my dad. She doesn't answer any of my questions, and asks nothing about me and my life.

My inner child is screaming for her lost mother. And the adult adoptee is screaming for her lost past.

Even though I understand that this must be hard for her just like it is for me, it still hurts. I thought everything would change now that she's back in my life. I thought she would give me all the answers I'd been searching for so long.

I thought I would learn something new about myself, beyond the impersonal and unreliable descriptions from the orphanage and SWS. Anything, just anything, even the smallest of details that would make me feel more than a number in a file, like a real human.

We start planning our trip to Korea. I write to my Omma again but months pass by without a reply. Korea has gone silent.

I'm starting to fear that she's disappeared. Or changed her mind. Or died.

In the meantime, Richey e-mails around to try and find out where my dad is buried.

No one seems to know anything, not even the police. Or SWS. Surprise, surprise.

I'm worried that we won't find him in time. I really want to find him so that I can say a first hello.

Hello, Dad. We never got a chance to meet...

but not one day has passed when I didn't think about you and wonder who you were.

And a last goodbye.

There's got to be some record of where people are buried.

It seems as hard to find dead people in Korea as living ones.

After almost six months of silence, I finally hear from Min-Jeong that my Omma has been in touch and wants to meet me when we come to Korea.

Oh, about time!

But she's wondering why you want to visit Korea. She's worried that you're not happy with your adoption.

What? How strange. But no, tell her not to worry. I just want to see the country where I was born and visit the places I stayed at.

As our trip approaches, there's a lot to prepare. Most things are not a problem.

I'm sorry, we don't have any Korean won. Do you want Hong Kong dollars instead?

I wish I could pack mountains of keepsakes to give my Omma. But there wouldn't be enough room for everything else in our luggage if I did.

Okay, Teddy and Poppy! I hope you're ready for a 30-hour flight. We're off to the airport and Korea!!!

We just wanted to call and wish you the best of luck on your trip! I hope all goes well. Say hi to your Omma and thank her for the loan.

Seriously, whatever happens, I'll always be your daughter.

Korea.
I'm back in the country where I was born.
Back in the country where I was abandoned.

Korea,
the country that sold me.

We were planning on staying at a hostel for adoptees, but instead we find ourselves in a taxi on our way to Min-Jeong's family. It's the middle of the night and we drive through a rainy Seoul.

We're exhausted after the long trip, but the kids are happy and excited. Everything feels slightly unreal.

Annyeong-haseyo! I'm Min-Jeong's mom!

Come in, come in! You'll get wet!

Min-Jeong's family is warm and welcoming, despite having unexpected guests at twelve-thirty at night in the middle of the week.

You and Poppy get my room, and Richey and Teddy get my brother's.

Oh, you're so kind! Are you sure about this?

Eat all you want, now! And welcome to Korea!

The first week, we have no plans or meetings, and so we take the children on endless walks, visiting beautiful parks and playgrounds, just taking Korea in.

Everywhere we go, we meet friendly and helpful people, eager to spoil the kids with treats and attention. We realize how unusual this is for us, that strangers aren't treating us as intruders. When people approach us in Sweden, it's usually to say something demeaning or to tell us off. There, our guard is always up, shoulders raised. Here, we can finally relax and just exist.

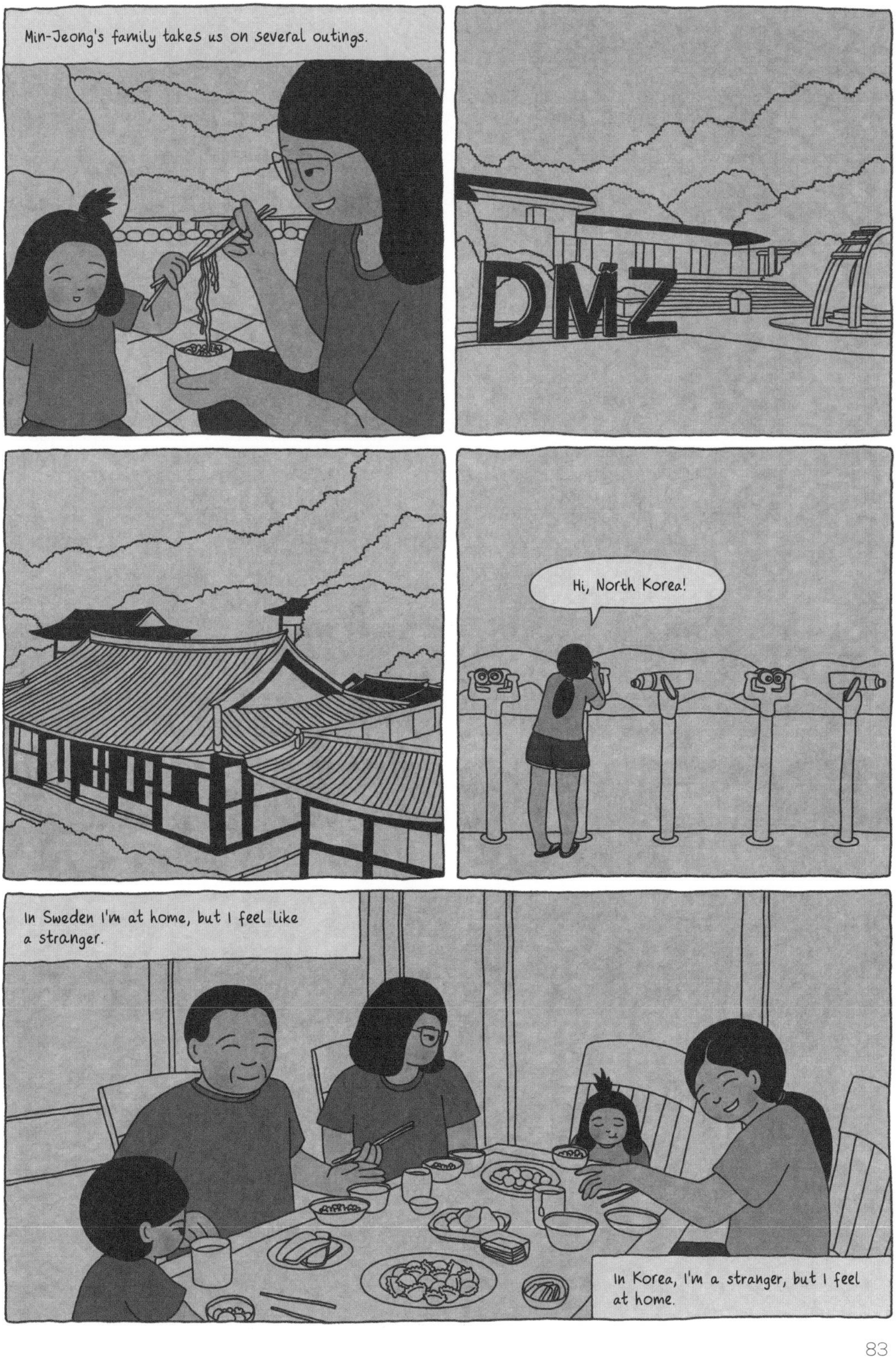
Min-Jeong's family takes us on several outings.
DMZ
Hi, North Korea!
In Sweden I'm at home, but I feel like a stranger.
In Korea, I'm a stranger, but I feel at home.

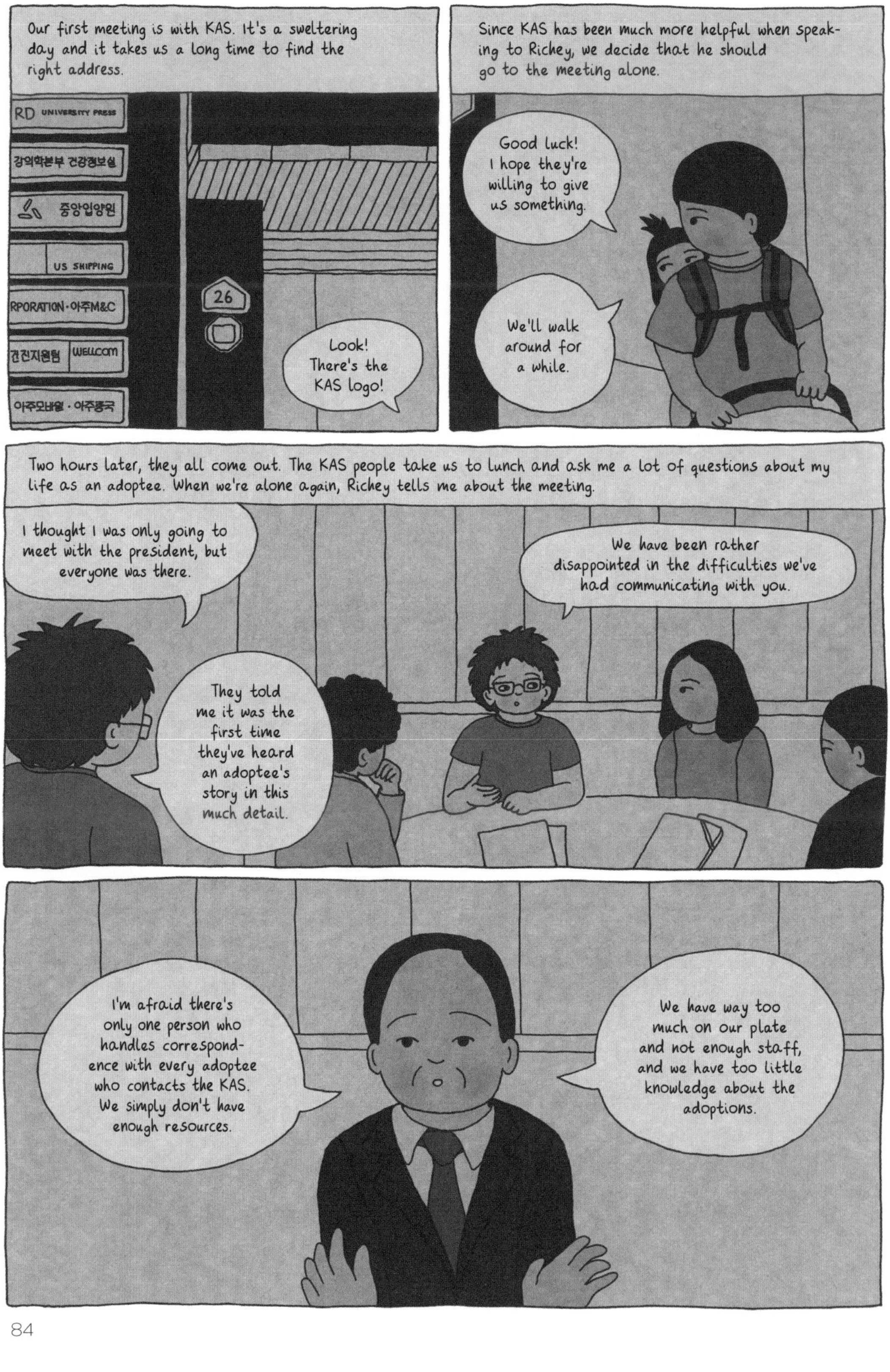
Our first meeting is with KAS. It's a sweltering day and it takes us a long time to find the right address.
RD UNIVERSITY PRESS
중앙입양원
US SHIPPING
RPORATION·아주M&C
WELLCOM
26
Look! There's the KAS logo!
Since KAS has been much more helpful when speaking to Richey, we decide that he should go to the meeting alone.
Good luck! I hope they're willing to give us something.
We'll walk around for a while.
Two hours later, they all come out. The KAS people take us to lunch and ask me a lot of questions about my life as an adoptee. When we're alone again, Richey tells me about the meeting.
I thought I was only going to meet with the president, but everyone was there.
We have been rather disappointed in the difficulties we've had communicating with you.
They told me it was the first time they've heard an adoptee's story in this much detail.
I'm afraid there's only one person who handles correspondence with every adoptee who contacts the KAS. We simply don't have enough resources.
We have way too much on our plate and not enough staff, and we have too little knowledge about the adoptions.

I showed them your contradicting documents and told them which ones we've had trouble acquiring.

And I asked them if they knew about Mr. Jung and Busan Children's Guidance Clinic.

A Mr. Jung, you say?

No, afraid not.

They told me that the president of KAS has adopted children himself, and that one of the staff used to work for Holt.* I wonder how this affects their work with helping adoptees.

But the most important discovery came when I asked about the search for your parents.

Search? No, we don't search for parents at all. The agencies do that as they have the resources. We only act on behalf of the agencies. For example, when they ask for a specific document, we make an official request for it.

So I don't understand why you tell adoptees that you're searching when you're not. You have to understand the consequences. You are actually preventing reunions.

We're like a toothless tiger. We can't search because we have no resources. Our role is to acquire documents, but unfortunately we seldom get what we ask for.

I wonder how these people who work in direct contact with adoptees can know so little about adoption and adoptees' lives! It should be a requirement that they have a clue.

They don't care at all about adoptees. This is just a job for them. They don't understand that what they are doing—or what they are not doing—has a direct impact on our lives.

Korea never thought we would return.
The country abandoned us before we
could speak up for ourselves.
No one knew that we would thirst for our
families and roots, that against all odds,
we would come back to live here again.
No one was prepared for adult adoptees to
come back and reclaim our rights.

The next day, we go to SWS, the agency that handled my adoption, and produced records that erased my background and chopped off my roots. The agency that turned me from a person with a history to a number in a file. As we enter the building, the first thing we see is the maternity ward.

I wonder how many mothers have given birth here in secret. I wonder how many are giving birth here right now.

How convenient, to have a maternity ward in your adoption agency

There are posters and brochures everywhere, with pictures of happy families and messages of love. There is no indication that it could be painful to give away a newborn baby. The fact that adoption requires families to be broken is a well-kept secret.

"Adoption is a second childbirth. It is a great and deep happiness borne by the 'love' that is thicker than blood. We wish that all children in the world would be happy in the bosom of their loving family.*

Both here and in Sweden.

There's an American adoptive family here too. The kids are laughing and singing nursery rhymes. I wonder how they feel. Did they start asking questions about their roots too? Or was it the parents' idea to take them to Korea?

Hee Sun takes us to a little room, full of portraits of adoptees and gifts from grateful adoptive families.

When Hee Sun comes back with a thick folder, I'm excited. Maybe I'll finally get answers to the rest of my questions about my adoption.

But I find a piece of paper that I'd forgotten about for all these years. It's strange but familiar. The insecure handwriting takes me back. It's the letter I wrote to SWS when I was searching for my parents as a teenager.

Dear Social Welfare Society

My name is Lisa Sjöblom
(Chung, Wool Rim).
I'm a girl, sixteen years of age. I have two parents and an older brother. He's also adopted from Korea.
I'm studying at highschoollevel and in the future my wish is to become a journalist.
In my sparetime I'm playing the piano, read a lot of books, paint and I like writing.

My wish is to know how my natural parents lives are today, what they are doing and so on.

If it is possible I'd like to make contact with them

Someday I'm planning to come and visit Korea, and see how it looks.

Your sincerely

Lisa Sjöblom
(리사)

What a broken person I was back then. What if she'd known what I know now.

Would I have felt as bad if they had found my family back then?

The doors are always locked here. If you want to leave the building you have to sign an agreement saying you will not attempt suicide again.

I have to examine your bag too. We don't allow any sharp objects.

I realize that SWS probably never searched for my parents back in the nineties. Adoptionscentrum told me everything that SWS had done to find them, but if it was true they would have succeeded. My documents had been available in Busan City Hall for all these years. Information about my mother and her family was just waiting to be found.

If they had wanted to find my parents, they could have, and I wouldn't have had to live with this relentless pain for all these years.

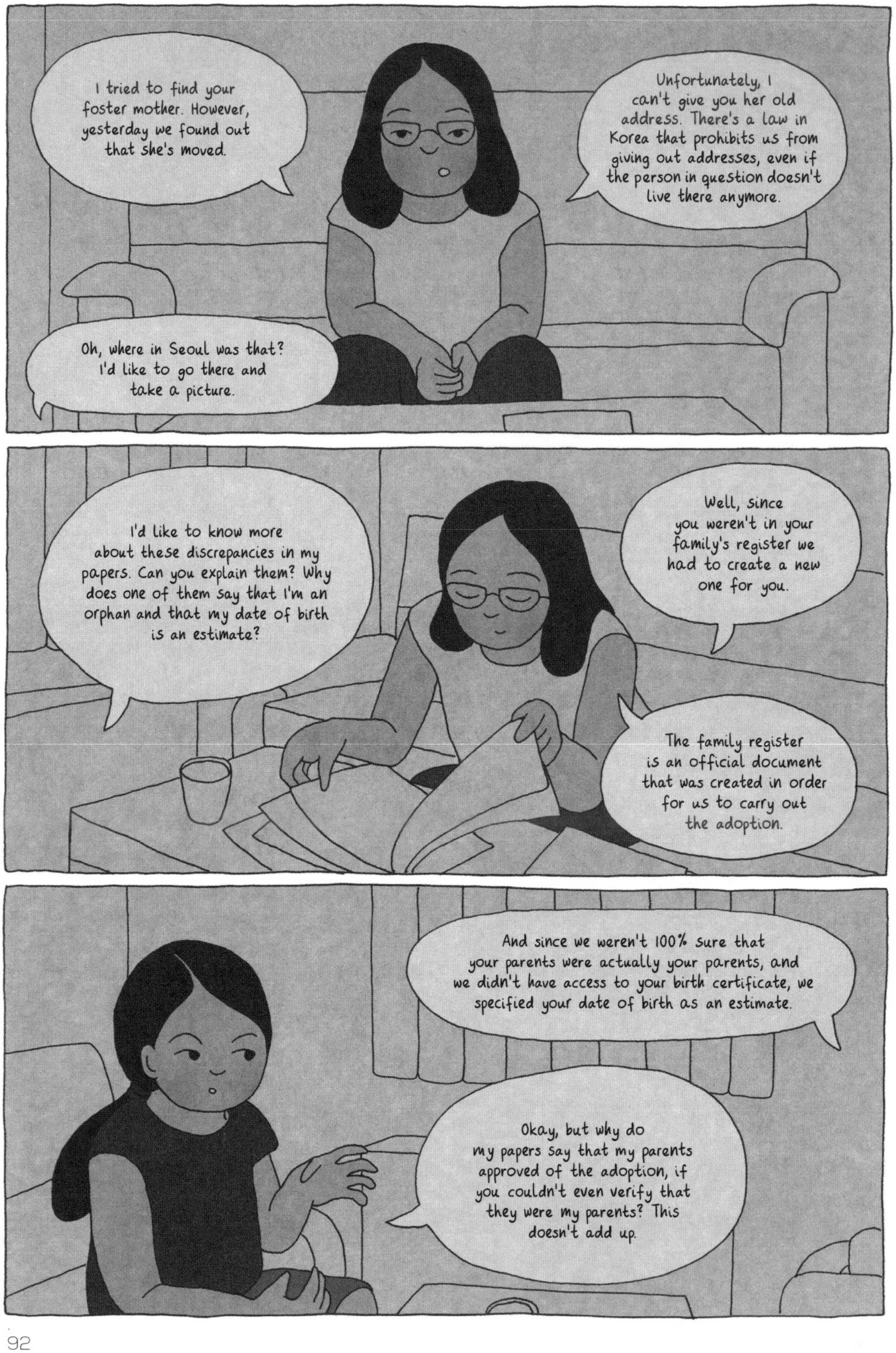
I tried to find your foster mother. However, yesterday we found out that she's moved.
Unfortunately, I can't give you her old address. There's a law in Korea that prohibits us from giving out addresses, even if the person in question doesn't live there anymore.
Oh, where in Seoul was that? I'd like to go there and take a picture.
I'd like to know more about these discrepancies in my papers. Can you explain them? Why does one of them say that I'm an orphan and that my date of birth is an estimate?
Well, since you weren't in your family's register we had to create a new one for you.
The family register is an official document that was created in order for us to carry out the adoption.
And since we weren't 100% sure that your parents were actually your parents, and we didn't have access to your birth certificate, we specified your date of birth as an estimate.
Okay, but why do my papers say that my parents approved of the adoption, if you couldn't even verify that they were my parents? This doesn't add up.

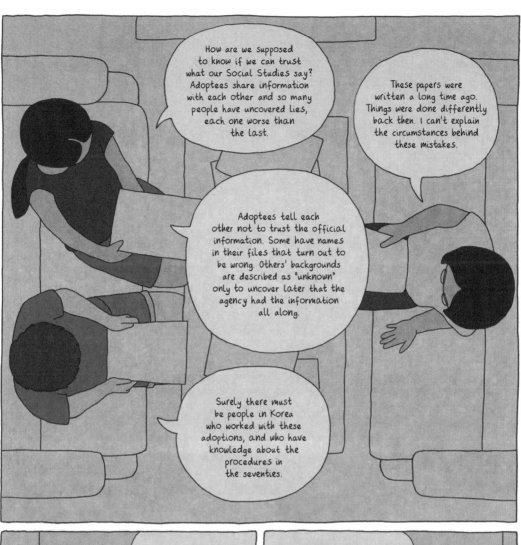

How are we supposed to know if we can trust what our Social Studies say? Adoptees share information with each other and so many people have uncovered lies, each one worse than the last.

These papers were written a long time ago. Things were done differently back then. I can't explain the circumstances behind these mistakes.

Adoptees tell each other not to trust the official information. Some have names in their files that turn out to be wrong. Others' backgrounds are described as "unknown" only to uncover later that the agency had the information all along.

Surely there must be people in Korea who worked with these adoptions, and who have knowledge about the procedures in the seventies.

Like Mr. Jung at Busan Children's Guidance Clinic. There must be someone who knows him and the institution that SWS was working with. His name is even in my papers!

I read your papers a hundred times to see if I could find anything relevant. But there was nothing at all about Mr. Jung. Or the place where he worked.

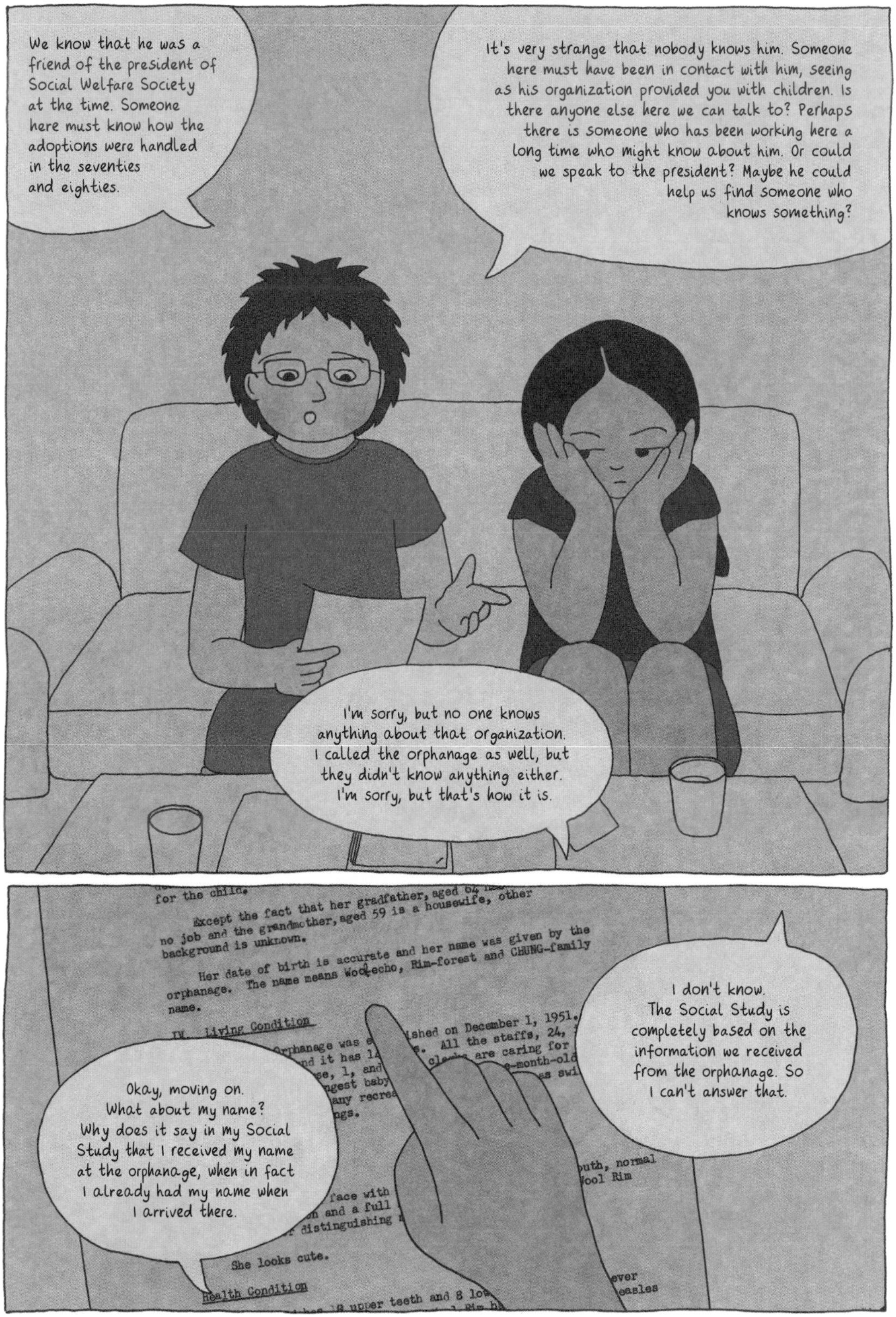
We know that he was a friend of the president of Social Welfare Society at the time. Someone here must know how the adoptions were handled in the seventies and eighties.
It's very strange that nobody knows him. Someone here must have been in contact with him, seeing as his organization provided you with children. Is there anyone else here we can talk to? Perhaps there is someone who has been working here a long time who might know about him. Or could we speak to the president? Maybe he could help us find someone who knows something?
I'm sorry, but no one knows anything about that organization. I called the orphanage as well, but they didn't know anything either. I'm sorry, but that's how it is.
for the child.
Except the fact that her gradfather, aged 64
no job and the grandmother, aged 59 is a housewife, other
background is unknown.
Her date of birth is accurate and her name was given by the
orphanage. The name means Wool-echo, Rim-forest and CHUNG-family
name.
IV. Living Condition
She looks cute.
Health Condition
Okay, moving on. What about my name? Why does it say in my Social Study that I received my name at the orphanage, when in fact I already had my name when I arrived there.
I don't know. The Social Study is completely based on the information we received from the orphanage. So I can't answer that.

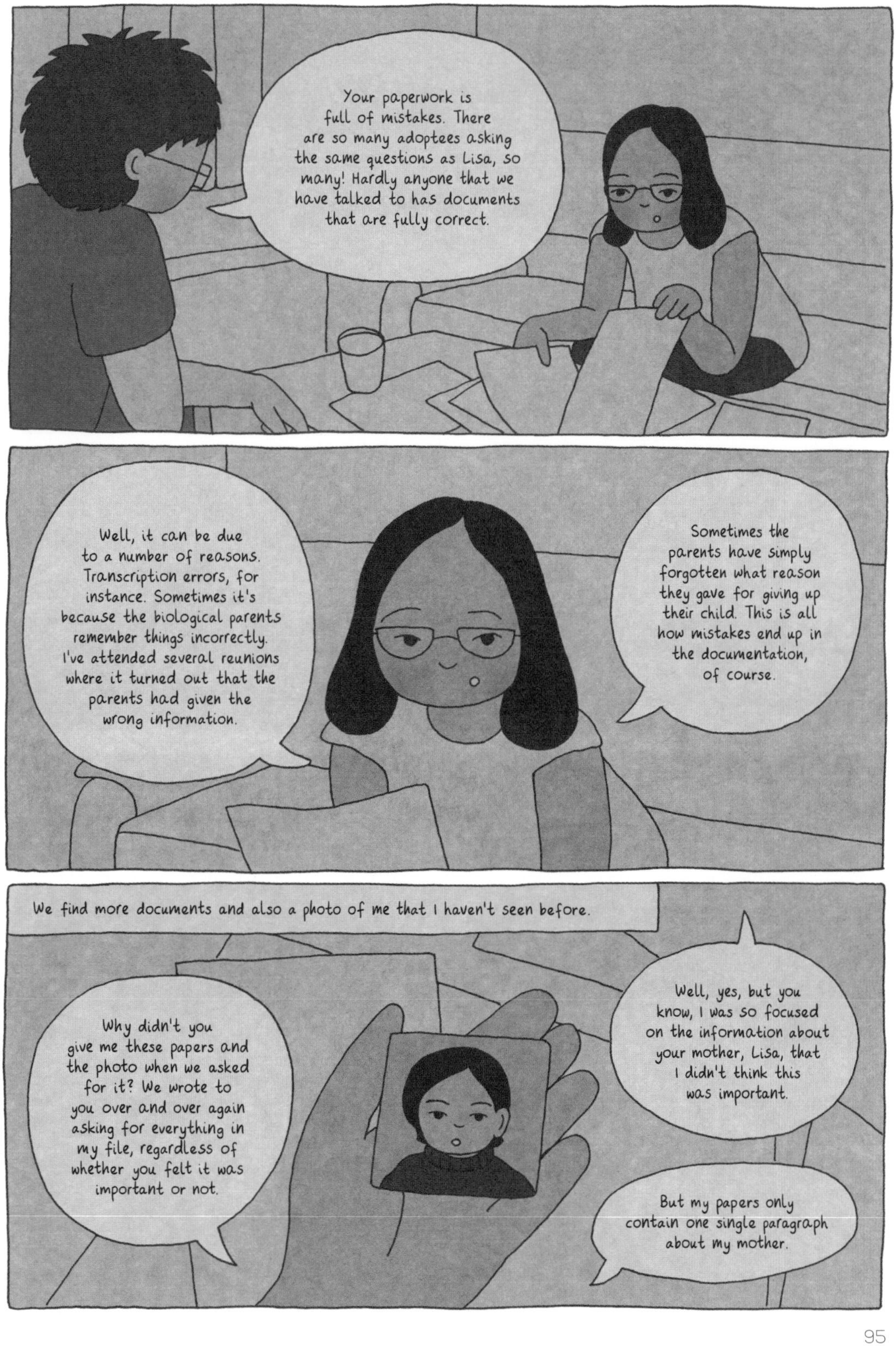
Your paperwork is full of mistakes. There are so many adoptees asking the same questions as Lisa, so many! Hardly anyone that we have talked to has documents that are fully correct.
Well, it can be due to a number of reasons. Transcription errors, for instance. Sometimes it's because the biological parents remember things incorrectly. I've attended several reunions where it turned out that the parents had given the wrong information.
Sometimes the parents have simply forgotten what reason they gave for giving up their child. This is all how mistakes end up in the documentation, of course.
We find more documents and also a photo of me that I haven't seen before.
Why didn't you give me these papers and the photo when we asked for it? We wrote to you over and over again asking for everything in my file, regardless of whether you felt it was important or not.
Well, yes, but you know, I was so focused on the information about your mother, Lisa, that I didn't think this was important.
But my papers only contain one single paragraph about my mother.

You hope that retracing your roots will give you some answers, but it only leads to more questions.

Can you tell me anything about the woman who was my escort? Do you know how that part was done? How were the escorts chosen? Who worked as escorts?

I'm sorry, but we don't have any information about them. And there's nothing about it in your papers either.

What about the search? Can you tell me more about what SWS has done?

SWS hasn't searched at all, we're not allowed to. Korean adoption law prevents us from doing that.

What? Not at all? But hasn't SWS arranged reunions before?

You know, I contacted KAS several times about your case. They told me they couldn't find your parents.

But they weren't searching either! They said that they needed direct instructions from you. They told us that they don't actually do searches at all. So they didn't even try.

What, they didn't even try? When did they say this? Have you talked to them?

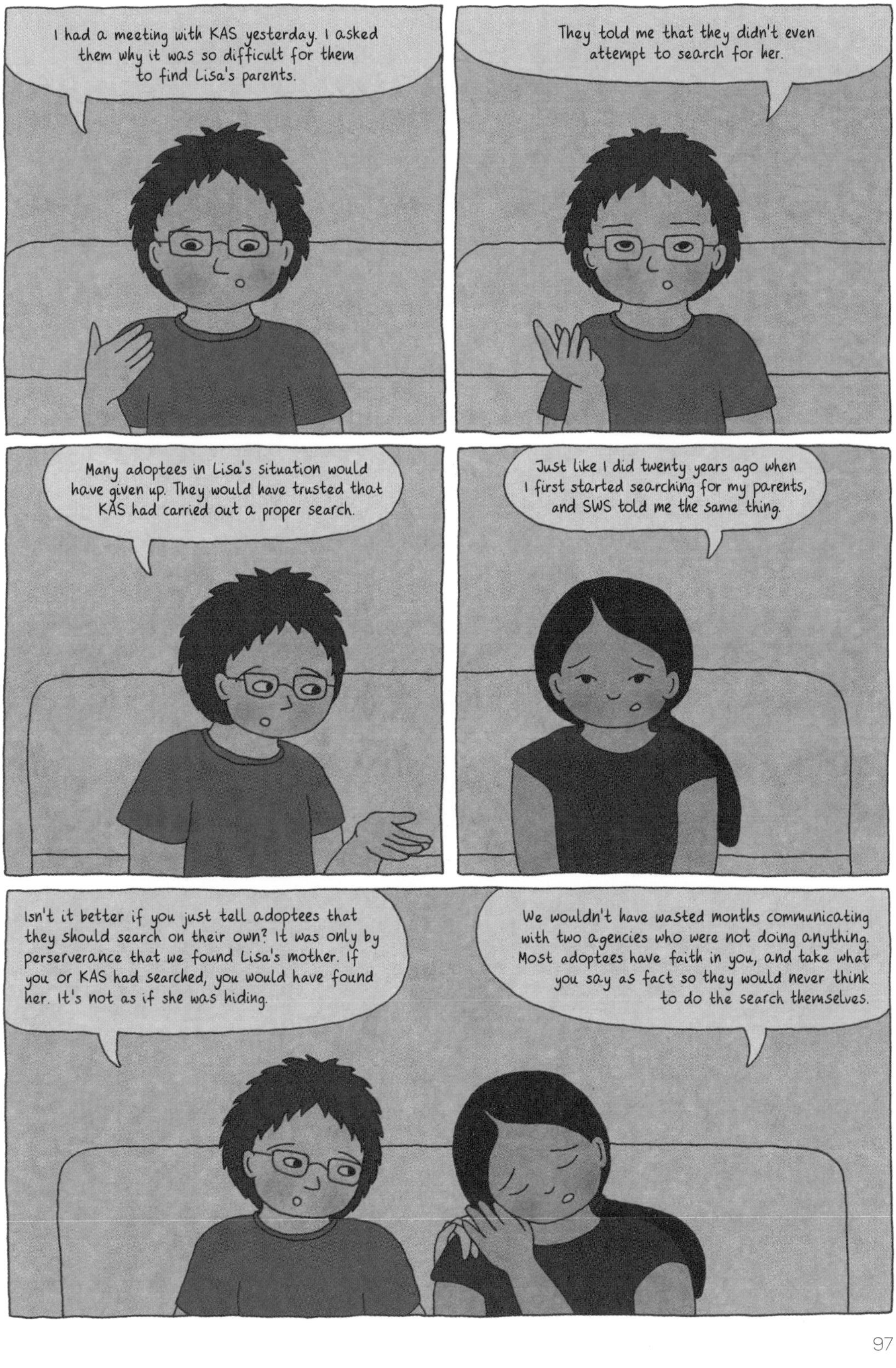
I had a meeting with KAS yesterday. I asked them why it was so difficult for them to find Lisa's parents.
They told me that they didn't even attempt to search for her.
Many adoptees in Lisa's situation would have given up. They would have trusted that KAS had carried out a proper search.
Just like I did twenty years ago when I first started searching for my parents, and SWS told me the same thing.
Isn't it better if you just tell adoptees that they should search on their own? It was only by perserverance that we found Lisa's mother. If you or KAS had searched, you would have found her. It's not as if she was hiding.
We wouldn't have wasted months communicating with two agencies who were not doing anything. Most adoptees have faith in you, and take what you say as fact so they would never think to do the search themselves.

I understand that many people are involved in this, but there's a big difference between finding out that someone has tried without success than finding out no search was even started.

It would have been better if you had applied for a family search with KAS first, instead of with us, we only relay information between KAS and adoptees.

But you have information about post-adoption services on your website!

With a link to a form for root searching with SWS! Why not link directly to KAS?

At KAS, they told us that they have to procure specific instructions from SWS or the other agencies before they can do anything. They also said that they usually don't even obtain the documents they ask for, since they lack authority.

We're not getting anywhere, and after two hours, the meeting is finished.

This is totally pointless. We're not going to get any answers.

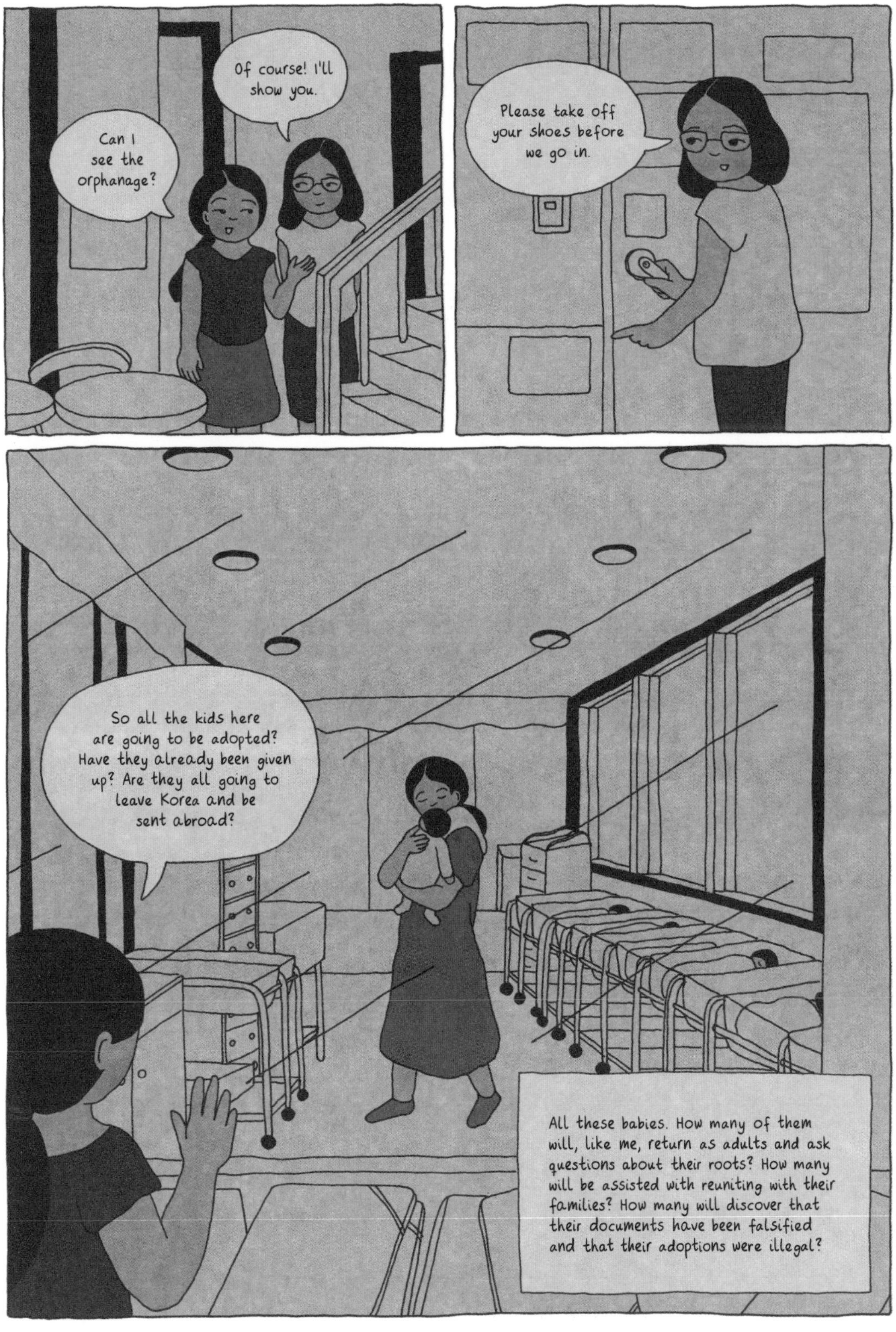
Can I see the orphanage?
Of course! I'll show you.
Please take off your shoes before we go in.
So all the kids here are going to be adopted? Have they already been given up? Are they all going to leave Korea and be sent abroad?
All these babies. How many of them will, like me, return as adults and ask questions about their roots? How many will be assisted with reuniting with their families? How many will discover that their documents have been falsified and that their adoptions were illegal?

Social Welfare Society:
the adoption agency that
makes every effort to portray a
one-sided narrative of adoption
as a positive way of starting
a family.

Social Welfare Society:
where thousands of parents
have come and returned home
childless. Their orphangage
reminds me that behind every
adoption is a family torn apart,
never to see each other again.

It's Midsummer's Eve back home, but I have another reason to celebrate.

Can I go like this? Or should I change?

I want to wear something I like. I'll remember what I wore tonight for the rest of my life! And we'll probably take a lot of pictures...

Min-Jeong, how should I greet her? Should I bow? Shake hands? Give her a hug? Should I try to say something in Korean?

What did she sound like on the phone? Is she nice? Oh, there are so many questions!

Haha, um, she sounded very strong-willed. Like a typical Omma who knows what she wants.

...like a typical Omma, but not to me. Only to my two little siblings who don't know they have a big sister.

Are you ready to go?

I wish it wasn't so hot. I wish my shoes weren't so uncomfortable. I change my mind about the dress and wish I'd worn my regular clothes instead of trying to look smart.

I really want my Omma to like me. I don't want her to be disappointed when she sees me.

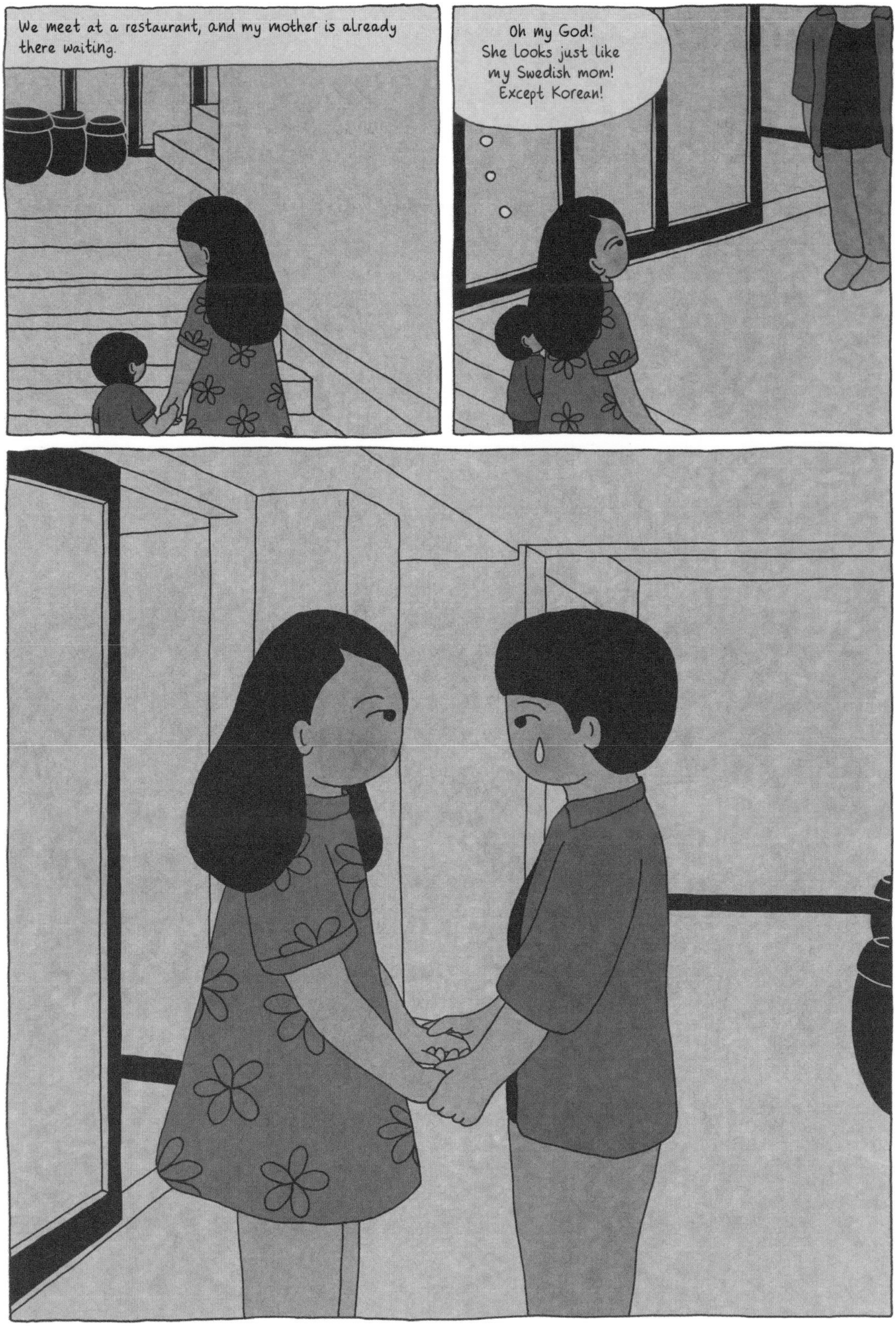
We meet at a restaurant, and my mother is already there waiting.
Oh my God! She looks just like my Swedish mom! Except Korean!

I'm so glad you are in such good health. I didn't eat well during the pregnancy and you were so small and feeble, I thought you weren't going to make it. I always thought you didn't.

Did you hold me after giving birth?

Yes I did, but I was very sick.

I was twenty when I had you. Your dad and I weren't together. It was just a fling. He was very popular, and everybody wanted to be with him.

So my Omma is four years older than my Social Study says.

I used to think that if I got married and had children as soon as possible, it would numb the pain from losing you. You've always been in my thoughts.

I want you to know that you come from a good family— educated and creative.

I can't stop looking at her. I'm looking for similarities and it feels just like the first time I saw my own children.

Someday I want to tell your siblings about you. But I don't know how.

There's so much at stake.

I didn't give birth at a regular maternity ward. I had to have a C-section, and they did it without anesthetic. I got very sick and it still gives me pain. It was your grandmother who gave you away.

Before I had my kids, I used to say that if I ever were to have children, my biggest fear would be that I would leave them, since my life began with me being abandoned. I thought it may be hereditary. But when I hear my Omma talk about my first few days, I realize how complicated the situation was. I'm ashamed I ever thought she just gave me up in cold blood.

After Wool Rim's grandmother passed away, I kept having these dreams about a boy and a girl, night after night. When I saw Teddy and Poppy, I realized it was them I had been dreaming of.

When I saw the pictures you sent me of them, the dreams stopped. I think it was my mother who sent them.

Omma, was it you who gave me my name? In my adoption papers it says that I got it at the orphanage, but in the paperwork from City Hall it says that I already had it before I arrived there.

No, it wasn't me. When the police called me about you, it was the first time I heard your name.

I wonder who it was then. It must have been someone who knew my background, since I got my father's family name.

It turns out she wasn't looking for me. The police suggested to her that I needed to hear this. My body hurts. None of the information I receive ever turns out to be true and the lies keep piling on top of each other. My files contradict each other, my mother contradicts the files. I don't know who to believe.

Min-Jeong, can you tell her that I don't need to be protected by any more lies. I already know the harshest facts about my life. Nothing is too hard for me to hear.

I just want to know about my first two years of life.

A few minutes later, my Omma drops the biggest bombshell of the evening.

Wool Rim, your father isn't dead. He's alive.

It was the policewoman who told me to say he was dead, so you wouldn't ask more questions about him.

I asked her not to try to find him. He has no idea about you. I was trying to protect him, but she looked for him anyway.

When I read your letters with questions about your father and where he is buried, I had to tell you. I know you won't stop asking until you get answers.

He's married and has two teenage boys. You look just like him.

I was very much in love with him, but he didn't care about me at all.

He's also from a good, well-educated family. So you come from two very good families.

And just like that, I'm a big sister to four people!

We go home and put the kids to bed, and then Min-Jeong, my Omma, and I go to a cafe to talk some more.

Reunions are not like the movies. You spend a lot of time waiting for translations.

You sit there waiting expectantly, envisioning what they're saying, and hoping that they're about to tell you the answer to the mystery of life.

Eventually my Omma shuts the door and closes herself off. She doesn't give more details about our shared history.

Your Omma was just telling me the plot of a film she saw the other night.

She's sitting right there, the woman I've been longing for from the moment we were torn apart. I just want to drown in her arms.

I'm imagining her being my mother, and I her daughter, and how we, in a stroke of magic, get every one of our lost years back.

If we could speak the same language, I would tell her all about everything that hurt.

Many adoptees sink one by one. Many of us take our own lives. Many more of us have tried. Many of us have been abused, some even murdered by our adoptive parents. Many of us are rejected, abandoned again for not fitting into our new families. Many of us are so, so lonely.*

If we could talk to each other, I could tell her why I turned out the way I did.

Sssh, it's all right. It's going to be okay.

Life as an adoptee can be hard. We feel like outsiders our whole lives. We desperately struggle for someone to listen to us, some-one who won't take our experiences away from us. We hear, more often than not, that what we are feeling is wrong.

It's too late for us to be mother and daughter. And the language barrier makes it impossible to be close.

Omma drives us home. I know I should be very happy, but the distance between us makes me feel a strange emptiness.

I'll see you in Busan in a few days!

Richey and I are up half the night, going over details about my Omma and my time in Korea. There are still a lot of question marks. Much of what we do know doesn't seem all that reliable. I hope to find out more when we travel to Busan and meet the police. I'm also hoping my Omma and I can take a DNA test there, so I can find out whether or not she actually is my biological mother. The uncertainty is killing me.

· Omma is several years older than what is said in my papers. The explanation given to us is that it was common in the past for children to die before the age of two (which is why people in Korea celebrate their child's 100-day "anniversary"). Because of this, parents sometimes didn't register their child's birth until they were as old as five, and consequently, the date of birth would sometimes be wrong. But my Omma's birth was already registered when her information was entered into my papers, so there shouldn't be a discrepancy between her actual age and the one that was registered. Richey and I suspect that presenting my Omma younger than she really was (my Social Study says she was sixteen when she had me) was done purposely to make her seem more vulnerable.

· One of Omma's first names is not the same as in my papers. She says it's a common thing in Korea to change your first name. She did it in 2012.

· My parents' background story is wrong. The Busan City Hall documents are completely fabricated, and what my Omma told me in her letter was also false. My parents knew each other, but were not together, and I was conceived after they spent one night together.

· It was my grandmother who arranged for me to be brought to the orphanage. She died in 2012. It's an adoption classic to blame someone who is no longer alive, and who can no longer testify to what really happened.

· Omma said that my father was dead, and when we talked on the phone I was told that he died while she was pregnant with me. However, in the letter she said that he had died after I was born. Now we know that he's actually alive. When the police found him he didn't want to acknowledge me. Later he said that he wasn't ready to meet me. His death was made up to protect his identity.

· My Social Study says that both my parents made the decision to give me up, and that they asked the orphanage to take care of me. This could not be true, since my father didn't even know he had a daughter.

· Considering how easy it would have been to just omit the father's name from my papers, it is strange that his name is both in the City Hall documents and the Social Study that were sent to my parents in Sweden. If my Omma had really wanted to protect his identity, she could easily have said that she didn't know or she could have given a false name. The access I had to his name made it possible for me to find him. Thanks to his name, the police in Busan could also look for him without my Omma's consent.

· My Social Study says that I got my name at the orphanage. I later found out that I already had the name when I arrived there, but now my Omma says that it was indeed the orphanage who named me. She tells me I was named Wool Rim because I used to scream so much, but she also told me that she hadn't heard my name before she spoke to Mrs. Kim. She didn't know which orphanage I was at, and there was no information about how I got my name at the orphange anyway, so how could she possibly know this?

· I was either born in a hospital that didn't have a maternity ward or obstetricians, or in a different part of the hospital as I had to be born in secret. This could also be why my hospital is impossible to trace. I was delivered by Caesarean section without anesthetic.

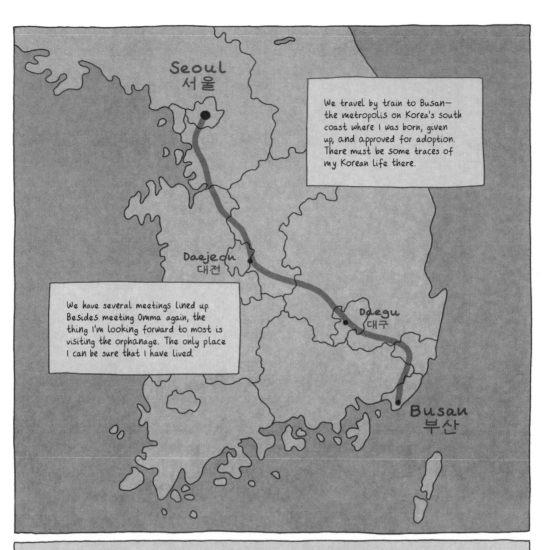

Seoul
서울

We travel by train to Busan—
the metropolis on Korea's south
coast where I was born, given
up, and approved for adoption.
There must be some traces of
my Korean life there.

Daejeon
대전

We have several meetings lined up.
Besides meeting Omma again, the
thing I'm looking forward to most is
visiting the orphanage. The only place
I can be sure that I have lived.

Daegu
대구

Busan
부산

When the kids are asleep, Richey and I discuss strategies for the meeting at Busan City Hall tomorrow, where
we hope we can extract some more new information.

Hello and welcome! Please follow me!

Can you ask her if we can see the document that they haven't sent us?

She says there aren't any more documents than the ones you've already received.

But one page is missing! The ones we received are marked 330, 331, and 333. Where's page 332?

Ah, but there's no information on that page. It's only a seal.

These sections were censored when we got them. May we now see what it says, since we've met Lisa's mother and know her background information?

We'd have to acquire approval from Lisa's mother to show you. Those sections have confidential details.

There's a special law here in Korea that doesn't allow us to disclose that information.

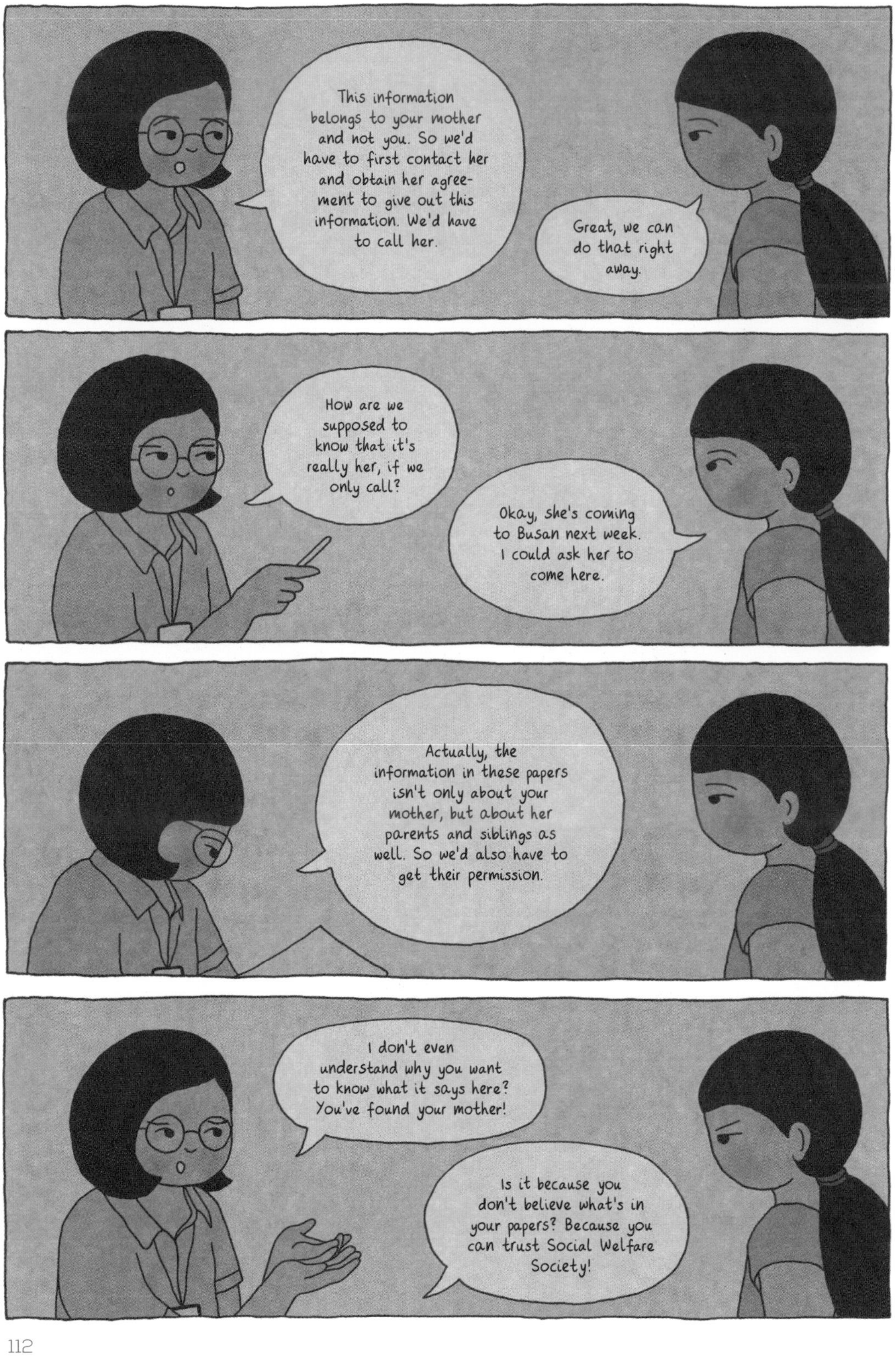
This information belongs to your mother and not you. So we'd have to first contact her and obtain her agreement to give out this information. We'd have to call her.
Great, we can do that right away.
How are we supposed to know that it's really her, if we only call?
Okay, she's coming to Busan next week. I could ask her to come here.
Actually, the information in these papers isn't only about your mother, but about her parents and siblings as well. So we'd also have to get their permission.
I don't even understand why you want to know what it says here? You've found your mother!
Is it because you don't believe what's in your papers? Because you can trust Social Welfare Society!

It doesn't matter why! I want to see all the information there is about me! This is all that's left of my life in Korea, and I have a right to know. When you know nothing, even the smallest detail is significant.

My papers are the only things I have from the first few years of my life. Many adoptees who have found their families later discovered that what was in their papers was complete fiction. It's important that we find out the truth!

I really don't understand why this is so important. All of this belongs in the past.

It's not just that. It's about gathering information about adoptions in general. So many of us are seeking answers, trying to understand the process of our adoptions. We're only told lies.

What document are you hoping to find, other than the ones you've already gotten? What piece is missing that you are so interested in?

All I want is every paper with the name Chung Wool Rim on it. They belong to me and I have a right to them.

These documents were created for the Mayor of Busan, to officially report an abandoned child. Once he got them, City Hall could decide where to place the child.

They were written by something called "Temporary Protection Shelter," so that Lisa could be placed at the orphanage.

Do you think Lisa's parents went there to arrange her relinquishment?

Someone must have met Lisa's mother to find out her back-ground?

This all happened such a long time ago. Things were handled differently back then. I don't believe any signatures were needed from the parents to leave a child. There were no procedures or rules to follow, and these things could happen in different ways.

Yes, is there a paper with their signatures where they officially confirm they're giving me up for adoption?

I'm guessing that those papers about Lisa's adoption would be either at the orphanage or in Social Welfare Society's archive, if they exist at all.

No, it wasn't them who handled it. It was another institution. In Lisa's papers it's called "Busan Children's Guidance Clinic," run by a Mr. Jung.

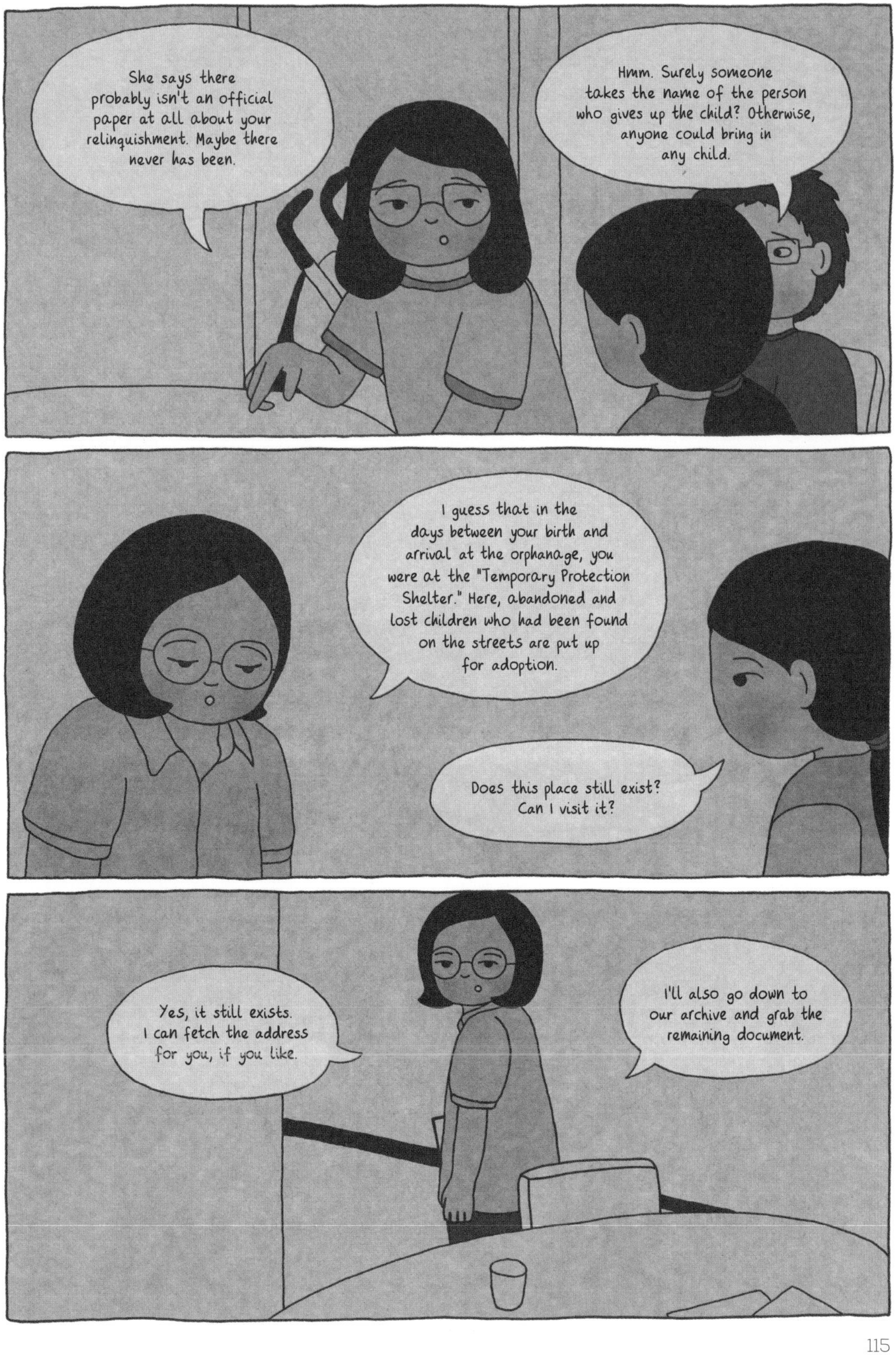
She says there probably isn't an official paper at all about your relinquishment. Maybe there never has been.
Hmm. Surely someone takes the name of the person who gives up the child? Otherwise, anyone could bring in any child.
I guess that in the days between your birth and arrival at the orphanage, you were at the "Temporary Protection Shelter." Here, abandoned and lost children who had been found on the streets are put up for adoption.
Does this place still exist? Can I visit it?
Yes, it still exists. I can fetch the address for you, if you like.
I'll also go down to our archive and grab the remaining document.

Finally we get the missing paper and it's true that it only contains a seal, but not just any seal—Busan Children's Guidance Clinic.

So what is Busan Children's Guidance Clinic?

You mean "Temporary Protection Shelter"? Because it's the same place. You can see it on the seal.

So you're telling us that the institution that takes care of abandoned and lost children is the same institution that approves children for adoption?

We'd like to visit this place, so could we please have that address then? Maybe there's somebody there who can help me put together the missing pieces of my life.

She changed her mind about the address and said that your records are from the hospital and that was where they were signed.

But she lied. She just wanted to stop you from visiting the shelter.

A pattern is emerging before us. All the documents that we really had to fight for have contained references to Mr. Jung and Busan Children's Guidance Clinic under various names.

And this organization is the same as "Temporary Protection Shelter," that is, the place where the police handed in lost children.

It's hard not to wonder how lost these children actually were. What was done to find their parents? How many of those taken into care were given papers that described them as given up or abandoned?

Papers with new names, new birthdates, and new identities, papers that turned them into adoptable orphans. Papers that enabled their adoptions to the West.

It sounds completely insane. But at the same time, it's now a familiar pattern. This is exactly how corruption within the adoption world is described.

Early every morning, we go to the beautiful Haeundae Beach, a stone's throw from our apartment.

One morning, Richey chats with a woman who wonders if I'm Korean. She's very moved when Richey tells her I'm adopted and visiting Korea for the first time.

We think we've found Lisa's mother, but they're going to do a DNA test to be sure.

So Lisa lived here in Busan for two years! And she's never met her family before!? My goodness!

Suddenly she gets up and asks us to come with her.

I run a gallery close by. I'd like to invite you to have Korean tea!

We have to do it now, because later I have to work!

We really weren't expecting this when we went to the beach this morning.

She treats us to an amazing traditional tea ceremony.

If it turns out she's not your real mom, I can be instead!

It's time to talk to Mrs. Kim again. Up until now, we've always managed to have our meetings while the kids were napping. This fails miserably today. They're crying and whining, and finally I have to take them for a walk to get them to calm down.

Phew! What a drama! But now they're finally sleeping.

Mrs. Kim was just about to tell us about how she found your mother. Sit down, I'll go and park the kids somewhere.

I started by looking for your maternal grandparents. At first, City Hall refused to provide me any information. But I didn't give up, and finally I obtained your mother's family register, and it matched the information you've supplied me. I found your mother's ID number and driving license, and that's when I saw that she'd changed her first name a few years ago.

I was thinking of how to approach her, since she has a new family. So I called her and started with a few little questions, just to see how she'd respond. Then I asked if she'd been pregnant and had a child when she was in high school. Well, she said she had, and that's when I told her that her daughter was looking for her.

The only ones who knew about her pregnancy were her and her mother. The documents from City Hall contain a completely fabricated story. But that's not unusual. Since there aren't any requirements to leave a background story, they're usually made up. It's possible that someone at Busan Children's Guidance Clinic wrote it, and that your mother didn't have anything to do with that document.

Mrs. Choi was silent most of the time, so I had the feeling she was the right person. I asked if she knew your name, but she didn't, so I told her your name was Wool Rim. I also told her you'd been adopted to Sweden. She didn't know that either.

This Mr. Jung and Busan Children's Guidance Clinic— we've tried to gather more information about them, but no one seems to know anything. Could you perhaps help us with that?

So Mr. Jung was involved in your adoption? I could definitely try to find him. I'll do some research and get back to you if I find anything.

Maybe your mother already told you this, but she gave birth to you in a hospital and not in a maternity ward. Your grandmother was a friend of the midwife who delivered you, and I think they must have arranged it beforehand.

These papers contain information about your family and relatives. You've got three uncles but one of them has passed away. And you've got two aunts and several cousins. Both of your maternal grandparents are also dead.

A big family tree is growing in front of my eyes, and even though I'm not in it, I know it belongs to me. It's mine, and also Teddy's and Poppy's.

Mrs. Kim then tells us how she located my father, using a similar method. No less than 30 people matched his details. He denied it at first when she asked if he ever had a daughter given up for adoption. He later called back to say it was possible.

New lies are surfacing. My father never consented to my adoption because he didn't even know that he had a daughter. How many adoptees have fathers who have no idea of their existence?

Your mother didn't want me to look for him. But I did anyway, since I was working on your behalf, and not hers.

For that reason, your mother wanted us to tell you that your father was dead. Hopefully, you'd stop searching for him.

But Omma said that it was your idea to tell me that!

When I found him, I showed his picture to your mother, and she confirmed that it was the right person.

Unfortunately, he's not ready to meet you. But maybe in the future.

He seems like a good man who has chosen family life over his career.

He's handsome too!

You've met him!!? You've met my dad!

Do you have a picture of him? Can I see!!!???

There it is—the second photo I've been waiting for all my life.

We look just the same.

I look like my dad. I look just like my dad! I have a dad and we look the same!

A couple of days later, we go by bus to visit Mrs. Kim and her family in a neighboring town. They take us to a restaurant in a traditional mud brick house.

A fantastic meal is laid out in front of us.

Well, I managed to find and talk to Mr. Jung.

At first I met his wife, who denied that Mr. Jung had anything to do with Busan Children's Guidance Clinic. When I showed her the photo of him together with your parents, she admitted that he had been the president there.

Afterwards, his wife took Mrs. Kim to the restaurant where Mr. Jung usually eats his dinner. Apparently, they eat out every day since Mr. Jung's wife refuses to cook for him.

Mr. Jung was silent for a long time, but finally he started to talk.

He told me that his role had been to sign forms approving children for adoption, but he felt deeply guilty about this, as he didn't feel it was right to send children abroad. So, in the end he quit his job. He and his family don't want to be reminded of those years, and they try to hide his past from friends and acquaintances.

Mr. Jung admitted that the institution had sold "found" children for adoption.

They received "donations," which were actually bribes from the adoptive parents.

Just as we suspected!

Many people were involved, Mrs. Kim continues, such as public servants, orphanages, and the adoption agencies.

When the agencies received requests from prospective adoptive parents, they got in touch with the orphanages. Once a suitable child was selected, the case was passed on to Mr. Jung for approval. An official report was written, and then the adoption was processed through the agencies. Everything appeared perfectly legal.

In order to approve a child for adoption, the child must have a guardian, which was usually the director of an orphanage or adoption agency. The child must have their own hojuk, which is a family register. If they didn't have one, one was created on behalf of the agencies.

A hojuk. It's one of those papers that says I'm an orphan and have no roots, despite the fact that I've always had a living mother and father in Korea. That's the paper that officially erases our backgrounds and turns us into empty pages with no history of our own.

Mr. Jung claims that he was never involved in any of the corrupt affairs himself. All he did was sign the forms that approved the adoptions. Everything else was done by his staff. Mr. Jung gave Mrs. Kim the name of his then secretary, who, according to him, was responsible for most of the corruption.

And here I was, thinking that maybe we were being too paranoid and reading too much into everything. But we were right! Our suspicions were right all along. Now the question is, how does my adoption fit in to all this? But it doesn't look like I will be getting any answers to this. Not on this trip.

Omma comes to Busan and to our apartment. She brings a suitcase full of gifts and clothes for all of us.

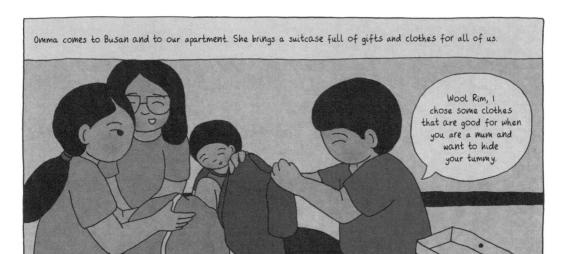

Wool Rim, I chose some clothes that are good for when you are a mum and want to hide your tummy.

Then she goes shopping, and starts cooking dinner. I'll finally get to taste Omma's cooking.

Ta-dah! What do you think?

Min-Jeong goes to take a shower and we're alone with Omma. I wish I could say something, but I don't know much more than "hi" and "nice to meet you".

After dinner, she insists on doing the washing-up and cleans the whole apartment. She's so much like my Swedish mother.

I promised your Omma not to tell you this, but she thinks you don't really trust her. That you think she's not the right person.

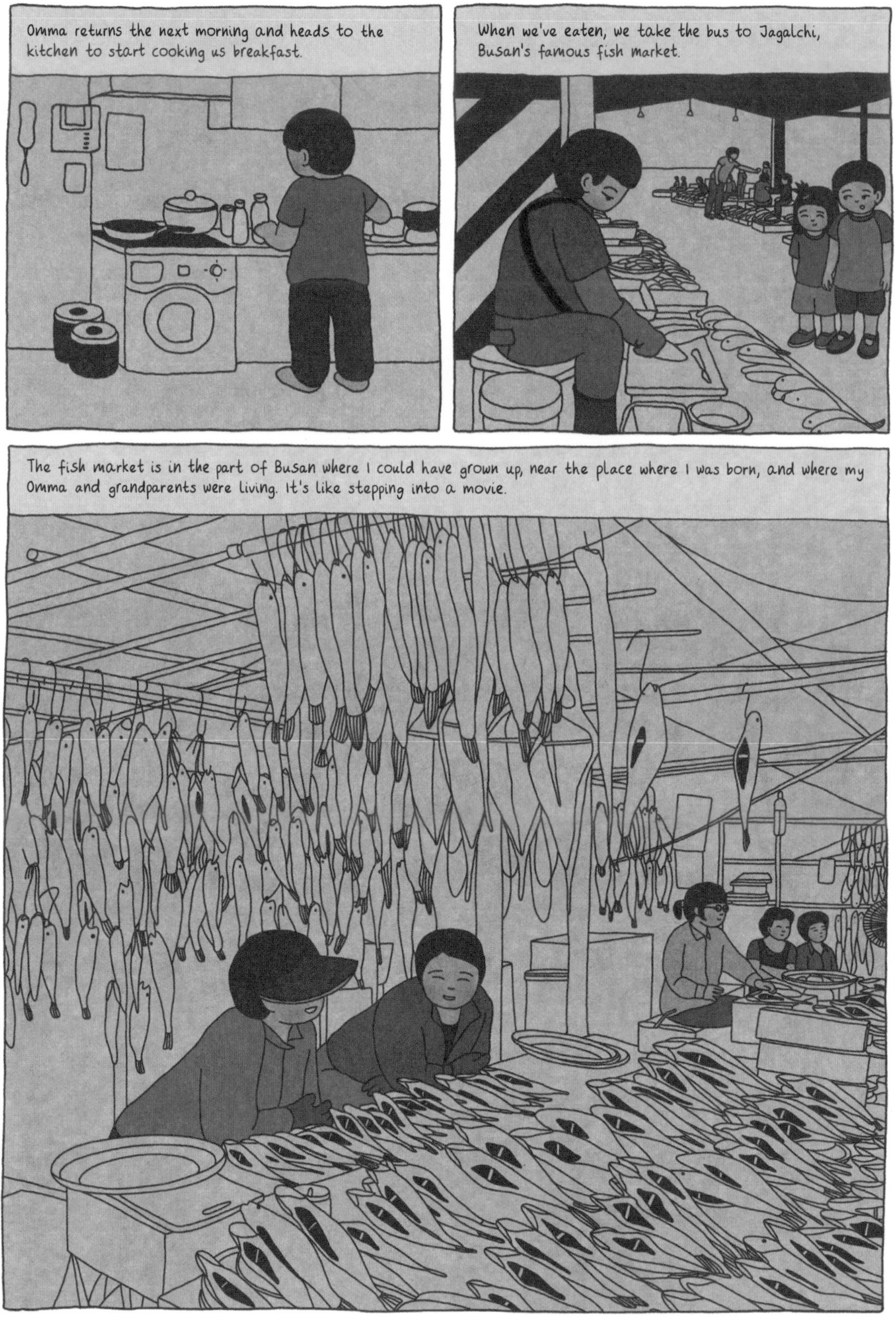
Omma returns the next morning and heads to the kitchen to start cooking us breakfast.
When we've eaten, we take the bus to Jagalchi, Busan's famous fish market.
The fish market is in the part of Busan where I could have grown up, near the place where I was born, and where my Omma and grandparents were living. It's like stepping into a movie.

After the market, we walk towards the area where Omma lived when she was pregnant, and where she gave birth to me. I'll finally see the part of the world where I took my first breath.

We're standing on the bridge that my Omma used to cross every day on her way to school. This could have been my route to school as well. This place could have been my home.

We're there, but at the same time we're far away.

The hospital where you were born used to be here. It looks different now, I don't recognize anything.

Omma, can we take a picture here?

We both look happy in the picture, but on the inside, I'm falling apart.

Okay, say KIMCHI!!

Can you ask Omma if we can look around the area? It would be nice to see a bit more.

Your Omma says she'd rather not. She prefers if we left now.

Richey and I run over to a little shop nearby, to try and buy some symbolic mementos.

We travel back in silence, and I wonder why my Omma wanted to leave so abruptly. Did some painful memories come back to life?

꿈만 같아요!

Your Omma says it's like a dream come true.

At last, the day has come to visit my orphanage. Mrs. Kim picks us up, and after a long car ride along winding roads, we're there.

It turns out to be the wrong orphanage. Unless we're mistaken, this place could be Mr. Jung's Busan Children's Guidance Clinic.

It makes me feel uneasy that it's in such a secluded location.

Hello! Please sit down. The director will be along in a moment. Can I get you anything to drink?

I'm trying to piece together all the facts about my life in Korea, and I wondered whether you had any records about me? Anything about my adoption, seeing that it was processed by you?

I'm afraid not. We don't have anything about you here. All our files have been digitalized, and nothing came up when I searched for your name. So I doubt that you've ever been here. You were probably moved directly from the hospital to your orphanage.

Nevertheless, Mrs. Kim has a long conversation with the man, and afterwards, she tells me what he said. We understand that it's not Mr. Jung's institution after all.

This place acted as a temporary shelter for abandoned children. The institution wrote a report to Busan Children's Guidance Clinic, who then found a suitable orphanage for the child.

The director thinks you were sent directly from the hospital to your orphanage. So your mother gave you up at the hospital. All the documents ought to be in City Hall. But it's possible they don't have those files anymore.

The mothers didn't come here themselves. Usually it was the grandmothers who came and filled out the paperwork. Forms were usually signed at the hospitals, some were even signed before the baby was born.

Your grandmother and the midwife knew each other, and your grandmother handled everything at the birth, including the forms. The midwife knew Mr. Jung, but unfortunately she died last year.

One by one, they've all died, the people who could've given me answers. A reminder of this painful race against the clock that just keeps ticking as you retrace your roots.

After lunch we continue to my actual orphanage. I'll finally be able to tread ground I've tread before.

The first thing we see when we enter the orphanage's office is a big poster with photos of missing children.

I wonder if many other adoptees have visited before.

I wonder what it feels like for the staff to meet us? Are they aware that we grow up, or do they just see us as little children?

The young staff working in the office show us to a table and I feel a reluctant uneasiness. What can they possibly know about how the orphanage was run in the seventies?

Here's the only document that we have about you. I'm afraid it doesn't say much.

Surely there must be something more in your archives? My adoption agency says that whatever's in my adoption papers is based on records from this orphanage. Descriptions of me as a baby, my parents' names, and details of my life here.

There was another director at the time you were here. When they got a new director, some old records were thrown away. It's possible that your files were among them.

But this is a scanned document. Is there some way I could see the original? It would be interesting to see what it looks like.

We'd have to ask the director.

Hello! I'm the director. I'm afraid that's not possible. We don't have your files anymore, except for the one we already gave you.

You see, this isn't the orphanage you stayed at. This one was built in 1987. Yours was close by, though.

Your records, along with many others, were destroyed in a flood that happened in the archive of the old building.

The papers could also have disappeared when we moved, or when we gave everything to the police for digitalization.

THERE IT IS!

Richey and can't believe our ears. We don't know how many adoptees have been told this exact thing when they've searched for their files.

1. Documents were lost
2. Documents were destroyed in a fire
3. Documents were destroyed by a flood
4. Documents were destroyed by a natural disaster
5. Documents were thrown away

Where's the old orphanage building? Is it a place we can visit?

No, I'm afraid not. It's been torn down and there's a motorway in its place.

There are no places left in Korea where I could have been. Korea has not only erased my past, it has erased everywhere I have ever set foot.

Do you have any photos left of the old building? Anything, so that I can see what it looked like when I was there?

No, I'm sorry, there's nothing left. We didn't keep anything when we moved to this building.

I got out the original document you asked for, and I also found all your files!

This man will always be one of my life's biggest heroes. He defied his boss and retrieved the files she had just told us did not exist. I wonder if he'll get to keep his job.

Why did they say that my documents were lost when they weren't? Why all these unnecessary lies one after the other?

Look! Another baby picture of me! It's even younger than the other photo they sent! Why didn't they send this? And why did they say there was only one document about me, when there was also this photo?

And there are different dates here too. Here it says you arrived on May 4th, and this other one says the 9th. I wonder which is correct.

In another book, we find a registry stating when the children were logged in by date of their arrival at the orphanage, and logged out on the date of their departure. Most entries have the note "international adoption" next to their name, with the name of the adoption agency. Many children aren't named, they are just a number. "+1 child to SWS," "+5 children to Holt." They aren't given a row of their own, but are simply added to another named child.

I wonder if it's these children Mr. Jung was talking about, the ones sold for adoption through bribes.

Oh my god, this is awful!

The remainder of our meeting is a familiar refrain. There are no lists of previous employees, no one we can contact who will tell us anything about the orphanage during the time I was there.

We have a look around the orphanage. It looks nice and it feels like the home of a large extended family. The older children are in school, and the younger ones are taught here.

I can't help thinking that taboo thought, that a life in an orphanage in my own country wouldn't have been worse than a life in a foreign one. The lives of these children are depicted as horrific, and are used as examples of why an orphanage isn't a home. But who decides that? Who decided that it's better for a child to lose everything—including their name—and be sent to the other side of Earth with their past erased.

When we look around, we meet an older woman who is a teacher for the smaller children.

Maybe we should ask her if she knows anyone who worked here in the seventies!

Yes, I do! I know a woman named Mrs. Kang. I can call her and ask if she wants to see you!

Mrs. Kang says she'd love to meet you! She asks if you're free tomorrow?

Oh, yes, of course!

All my hopes are now pinned on Mrs. Kang. She's the last chance I have of finding out anything about myself and my life here.

And tomorrow, Omma and I are taking the DNA test. Soon we'll know for sure if we're mother and daughter.

141

We meet Mrs. Kang next morning in the City Hall cafe.

I show her my baby and orphanage photos.

I don't remember you, but I do have memories that could relate to you. Like your name—Wool Rim. I remember a baby with that name who cried a lot. I thought she got a fitting name. It means "forest echo."

We sit down at a table and I ask a thousand questions about the orphanage. What did it look like? How many kids were there? How were we cared for? How did they pick a child out for adoption?

When I worked there, about three children a week were left on the steps of the orphanage.

Most of the children who arrived didn't have any background information, and some came with name tags around their necks.

I've never seen anyone with this much background information in their papers before.

I guess the person who gave you up really wanted you to find your way back to the family.

When the children first arrived, they would scream and cry uncontrollably. They'd cried for their mothers, traumatized by their abandonment. It usually took at least six months for them to start feeling secure, Mrs. Kang tells us.

Some children died, some disappeared in unexplained circumstances. About 20 children a month were sent for adoption, mostly overseas.

The older children who came had already been approved for adoption, so for them it was more like a foster home. They knew they were only going to be there for a short while.

The orphanage was very popular among the adoption agencies. It was like a production line for them. Every month they demanded a certain number of children, and that number kept increasing.

Many children who were adopted within Korea were returned to the orphanage. If their adoptive parents weren't happy with them, they'd just sent them back. They wanted flawless, healthy children.

The children were used to seeing other kids come and go, understanding their turn to leave the orphanage would come. When it did, they left in silence, without a tear, emotion, or any fuss at all, in stark contrast to their arrival.

When I worked there, I thought I was doing a good deed. I thought my work was something noble, and that adoption was the best option for the children who came to us. Today, I feel differently.

I keep in touch with several children who were under my care and sent for adoption. I've reconsidered. Now, I understand that adoption wasn't the best solution. Maybe we shouldn't have sent all those children away...

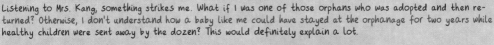

Listening to Mrs. Kang, something strikes me. What if I was one of those orphans who was adopted and then returned? Otherwise, I don't understand how a baby like me could have stayed at the orphanage for two years while healthy children were sent away by the dozen? This would definitely explain a lot.

Thank you for taking the time to see me!

It means so much to me! I'm so grateful!

Don't mention it, Wool Rim! I wish you the best of luck, and I hope all your questions are answered. And good luck with your DNA test. I hope your mother really is your mother!

After lunch with Mrs. Kang, we meet up with my Omma and Mrs. Kim outside of the police station. It's time for the DNA test.

I'm sorry, but I have to take a hair. It'll hurt a bit!

And now I'll scrape the inside of your cheek.

My Omma is visibly uncomfortable with the whole situation, but at least now we'll know for sure.

Is it okay if I just write "Wool Rim's mother" on the test? So that she can remain anonymous?

When we're done, it's clear that Omma is upset. I don't know if it's because of the test or something else.

I've really had enough!

We can't have a relationship if you don't let go of the past! There are no more answers to be had! Enough is enough!

But...

I...

She doesn't want to talk about the past anymore or answer any other questions. She asks me to stop digging; it should be enough that we've found each other. When we part, I understand that it's for good. Our plans for the future were a fantasy that none of us could live in. Our shared history is a painful black hole. Once again, I lose her.

I carry a dull ache in my chest for the last few days of the trip. I'm already mourning our departure. Busan may be the most fantastic place I've ever been to. It's hard to comprehend that this city was once a part of me, that this place bears my origins. Busan, my beautiful, wonderful, magical birthplace.

On our last night in Busan, Mrs. Kim and her daughter come to pick up some things she'd lent us, and to talk about some final, important details about the DNA test.

We don't have anyone to interpret, as Min-Jeong has returned to Seoul. So Mrs. Kim spends half an hour calling around, trying to find someone who can help us.

This language barrier is frustrating. Finally, Min-Jeong answers her phone.

Mrs. Kim has a consent form that you need to sign.

I've been trying to find Mr. Jung's secretary, but there is simply no trace of him.

He's impossible to find.

And I'm so sorry about you and your Omma.

I can't even begin to thank you for everything you've done for me and my family. Thank you for finding my Omma and thank you for taking me to the orphanage. Thank you so much!

I'm going to keep looking for answers for you. Stay in touch and let me know if there's anything else I can do. Now you take care!

We spend a lovely last few days together with Min-Jeong and her family.

A kiss for Min-Jeong!

On our last day in Korea, Min-Jeong's mom and aunt make our favorite dish, bibimbap. Richey has been trying to get tired of bibimbap so that he won't miss it back in Sweden. So far it hasn't worked at all.

How will we live without this food? I'm already having withdrawals!

Thank you for everything you've done for us! We came here to find a family, and we certainly did.

Saying goodbye is hard. What would this trip have been without Min-Jeong and her family?

Our trip to the airport feels surreal. I want the bus to turn around, or for something to happen that forces us to spend another night in Korea. Anything for one more day in this wonderful country. I don't want this to be my only trip to Korea; yet, the country slowly disappears behind us.

I have unanswered questions and I'm returning to Sweden with many more. I have a hopeless longing for my unknown siblings.

When will Omma feel comfortable enough to open up about the past? Will my siblings ever know they have an older sister? Will my dad ever want to meet me? The quest for your past is usually viewed as the end of a painful journey where an adoptee can finally find peace when they reunite with their family. For me, though, this is just the beginning of an uprising, of a rebellion.

It's been 35 years since I was adopted to Sweden. How little I was. How little I knew.

And now, I leave Korea once more...

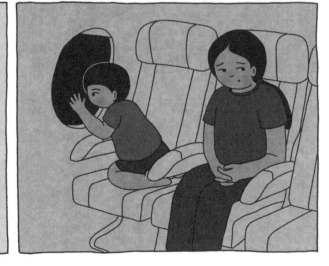

to once again arrive in a country where I'm a stranger.

Ni hao? Konichiwa? Where are you from?

At home, an e-mail from KAS awaits me.

Hi! We've got the result from the DNA test for Lisa and Lisa's birth mother. It shows with 99,997% accuracy that they are mother and daughter.

Congratulations!

And an e-mail from Mrs. Kim.

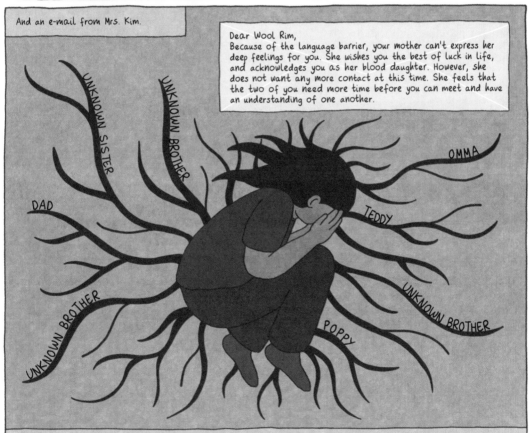

Dear Wool Rim,
Because of the language barrier, your mother can't express her deep feelings for you. She wishes you the best of luck in life, and acknowledges you as her blood daughter. However, she does not want any more contact at this time. She feels that the two of you need more time before you can meet and have an understanding of one another.

UNKNOWN SISTER
UNKNOWN BROTHER
OMMA
DAD
TEDDY
UNKNOWN BROTHER
UNKNOWN BROTHER
POPPY

There is a word in Korean culture—한/HAN—which describes the bottomless sorrow people feel after an enduring suffering, after having been wronged, persecuted, and oppressed. 한 is a part of Korea's cultural identity, and it comprises hope, despair, acceptance, and a resilient desire for revenge. At this very moment, another vulnerable family is currently being torn apart, another child is being dispatched to a distant country with faked papers, under false pretenses. For them we must bear witness.

151

POSTSCRIPT

All my life I have fought to tell my own story. It's always been there, but it's gone through many edits before it finally felt authentic. I still find it hard to express the sorrow I feel. But my anger can be heard loud and clear.

We risk it all when we loudly proclaim that our stories don't match up to what's expected from us. We put our family ties at risk, both old as well as new ones, and we suddenly find that we're alone, isolated between two cultures and two families. When we start to move outside the lines of what we, as adoptees, are allowed to say, when we deviate from the established and accepted narratives, and when we try to reclaim our lost identities, this is regarded as naiveté. It's seen as an expression of ingratitude and a questioning of, not just our own fates, but also everybody else's. This, I think, is one of the reasons why our stories are considered dangerous, even offensive, to other adoptees.

But it's essential that we tell these stories. It is necessary for us, for others, for our respective families, and for the adoption world that our voices are heard. There are more and more of us who share these stories with each other, and even more who go through the same torturous struggle. We're not fighting because we want to, but because we have to. We're fighting for our survival.

Everything I've read about adoption for most of my childhood, was written by adoptive parents or by people who work for adoption agencies. They've set the terms and standards for how we may or should understand our health, our attachment, the racism we're subjected to, our countries of origin, our first families, our adoptive families, our lives in Sweden, and our lives as children, which continue long after we've turned eighteen, since we're never fully allowed to grow up.

Now, many of us are adults. Many of us have children and grandchildren. Many of us have returned, some of us have reunited with, some of us have found out that the stories we grew up with have had gaping holes in them, filled with lies. We must be allowed to tell people about these lies without being dismissed as hateful, ignorant, or damaged. Adoptees all over the world deserve to be able to trust that the documentation about us is truthful; we deserve to know that our parents weren't coerced into giving us up, that our parents weren't tricked into signing false or misleading contracts. We deserve to know that we weren't kidnapped or sold.

We deserve access to our own stories and to speak with our own voices...

...no matter how we sound or what we say.

FOOTNOTES

pages 5–6 Authentic letter from Adoptionscentrum—Sweden's largest, and the world's second largest, adoption organization.

page 11 Poem by Fleur Conkling Heyliger.

page 14 My Korean name, "Wool Rim," is sometimes written with a hyphen and sometimes without. I was given the name "Wool Rim" in Korea, but a hyphen was added after my adoption.

page 22 Rothschild, Matthew, "Babies for sale. South Koreans make them, Americans buy them," *The Progressive*, 1988.

page 33 Several of the institutions here have other names today.

page 33 Examples of other middlemen: translators, lawyers, hotels, taxis, courts, hospitals, escort services.

page 34, panel 1 *Höjer, Dan & Lotta, Hjärtat mitt – En saga om adoption* ("Heart of Mine—a story about adoption"), Rabén och Sjögren, 2000.

page 34, panel 3 Wirsén, Stina, *Vems bebis?* ("Whose baby?"), Bonnier Carlsen, 2011.

page 34, panel 4 *Mjölner, Linda, Lilla Quains får en storebror* ("Little Quains gets a big brother"), Idus förlag, 2014.

page 35 The first time I read about this was in *Blod är tjockare än vatten* ("Blood is thicker than water") by Astrid Trotzig, Bonniers, 1996.

page 36, panel 3 The quote is from Jane Jeong Trenka's blog "Bitter Angry Ajumma" (jjtrenka.wordpress.com). [This blog is not available anymore]

page 36, panel 5 Quote from Unicef's website (www.unicef.org/media/media_45279.html).

page 37 Here is a selection of the headlines and keywords I've come across while googling "illegal adoptions." Many of the headlines and keywords lead to several different articles on the same subject. I've listed a few of them here.

Child laundering and intercountry adoptions: Smolin, David M., "Child Laundering: How the Intercountry Adoption System Legitimizes and Incentivizes the Practices of Buying, Trafficking, Kidnapping, and Stealing Children," *The Wayne Law Review*, Vol 52:113.

Operation Babylift: Mass evacuation of more than 10,000 Vietnamese children at the end of the Vietnam War (April 1975). Many of the children were adopted by Western families and were never reunited with their original families.

Illegal baby trade: Kapstein, Ethan B., "The Baby Trade," *Foreign Affairs*, November/December 2003 issue.

Child trafficking and Australia: Clair, Siobhan, "Child Trafficking and Australia's Intercountry Adoption System," Research paper for The University of Queensland Human Trafficking Working Group, 2012.

Guatemala's stolen children: "Guatemalan army stole children for adoption, report says," CNN, 2009.

The paper orphans of Nepal: *Paper Orphans*, documentary by Journeyman Pictures, 2013. Another documentary with the same name, *Paper Orphans*, directed by Marie Ange Sylvain-Holmgren, Terre des hommes, 2010.

Concern rising over illegal adoptions: "Concern rising over illegal adoptions," IRIN News, 2008.

Saving orphans or child trafficking: Voigt, Kevin, "International adoption: Saving orphans or child trafficking?," CNN, 2013.

Unicef warns of child trade: "Unicef varnar för handel med barn i katastrofens spår" ("Unicef warns of child trade in wake of catastrophe"), Swedish daily newspaper *Dagens Nyheter*, 5 January 2005. "Risk for Romanian child trade", Swedish daily newspaper *Svenska Dagbladet*, 15 November 2006. "Unicef varnar för handel med barn i Haiti" ("Unicef warns of child trade in Haiti"), Unicef, 22 January 2010.

Baby exporting nation: *Baby Exporting Nation: The Two Faces of Inter-Country adoption*, documentary by KBS In-Depth 60 Minutes, 2005.

The dark side of international adoption: "Pound Pup Legacy—exposing the dark side of adoption" is a website that continuously collects information about illegal and unethical adoptions (poundpuplegacy.org).

Living with dead hearts: *Living with Dead Hearts*, documentary about child kidnappings in China, by Charlie Custer & Leia Li, Songhya Films, 2013.

Illegal adoption as child trafficking: de Witte, Iara, "Illegal adoption as child trafficking: The potential of the EU Anti-trafficking Directive in protecting children and their original family from abusive intercountry adoption", master's thesis in European Studies, University of Amsterdam, 2012.

The stolen generation: "The Stolen Generations," adoptions of Aboriginal Australian children and children from the Torres Islands, who were forcibly taken into custody by the Australian government. This went on from the early 20th century until well into the 1970s. On Feb. 13th, 2008, the victims received a formal apology from former Prime Minister Kevin Rudd.

Child trafficking and adoption in Haiti: Vigo, Julian, "Child Trafficking and Adoption in Haiti," *CounterPunch*, 2013. Joyce, Kathryn, *The Child Catchers: Rescue, Trafficking, and the New Gospel of Adoption*, PublicAffairs, 2013.

Thriving market for illegal adoptions: "Illegal adoption," UNRIC In Focus, United Nations Regional Information Centre for Western Europe, Human Trafficking.

Irish Children Sold for Adoption: Björklund, Marianne, "På jakt efter en sann historia" ("Searching for a true story"), Swedish daily newspaper *Dagens Nyheter*, 17 June 2014. Sixsmith, Martin, *The Lost Child of Philomena Lee*, Pan, 2010.

page 38, panel 2 "Holt International's price for children," *Hankyoreh* 21 Cover Story, 24 July 2009.

page 38, panel 3 Joyce, Kathryn, *The Child Catchers: Rescue, Trafficking, and the New Gospel of Adoption*, PublicAffairs, 2013.

page 38, panel 4 Stuy, Brian H., "Open Secret: Cash and Coercion in China's International Adoption Program," *Cumberland Law Review*, Vol 44, No 3, 2014. Joyce, Kathryn, *The Child Catchers: Rescue, Trafficking, and the New Gospel of Adoption*, PublicAffairs, 2013.

page 38, panel 5 See among others the film Resilience by Tammy Chu, KoRoot, 2009.

page 38, panel 6 Dobbs, Jennifer Kwon, "Ending South Korea's Child Export Shame," Foreign Policy in Focus, 23 June 2011.

page 42, panel 1 "Holt International's price for children", *Hankyoreh* 21 Cover Story, 2009-07-24.

page 42, panel 3 The Facebook groups mentioned have approved of being named here.

page 42, panel 4 Authentic quote from Colombian adoptee Johanna Lundqvist.

page 42, panel 5 and 6 The ads are inspired by those found on Korea Adoption Service's website (www.kadoption.or.kr).

page 43 Dobbs, Jennifer Kwon, "Real Support for Unwed Moms," *The Korea Times*, 30 October 2009. The quote is edited for length.

page 50 The Swedish Social Insurance Agency pays a tax-exempt grant of 75,000 SEK to adoptive parents, in cases of approved international adoption.

page 83 Holt International, Korea's largest and oldest adoption agency, who together with Social Welfare Society have been criticized for repeatedly breaking Korea's own adoption law as well as violating the Hague Convention on Parental Responsibility and Protection of Children and the United Nations Convention on the Rights of the Child.

page 86 Quote from Social Welfare Society's magazine (recurring in several issues).

page 106 The Swedish governmental investigation "Adoption – till vilket pris?" ("Adoption—at what cost?") from 2003 shows that adopted people in Sweden run a 3,6% higher risk of committing suicide than non-adoptees. In the US, an estimated 10% of adopted children are subject to "re-homing", which means being relinquished by the adoptive family and adopted once more. Sometimes several times, and sometimes in completely illegal circumstances. Many of the children are advertized through social media (see Reuters Investigates, "The Child Exchange: Inside America's underground market for adopted children," 2013. Read more about racism against adoptees in the study Adoption med förhinder ("Adoption with Complications") by Tobias Hübinette and Carina Tigervall, Mångkulturellt centrum, 2008.

THANK YOU

RICHEY
*for your tireless detective work and
your never-failing support*

MIN-JEONG
*for your work as interpreter, even when exhausted and
when emotions were fraught. I also want to thank you
for your help with the Korean in this album*

MRS. KIM
(who in reality has a different name)
*for not giving up until you had found
both my parents*

JOHANNA
*for valuable feedback and proofreading, and for
lending a piece of your voice to the album*

MY ADOPTED FRIENDS
*who are always there for each other, and who
even in the hardest of times continue to fight for
the rights of adoptees and first families*

JOHANNES
for believing in my story and in this album

MY SWEDISH AND KOREAN PARENTS

TEDDY AND POPPY